Bulls, Broncs, & Buckles

A Collection of Short Stories and Vignettes

Mary McCashin

Special Thanks...

Editing by Janie Mims

Cover Illustration and design by Kelsey Steller

Cover photograph courtesy of Glenna Smith & Wild West Photography

At least once a day someone asks me how did I get here; how did a farm kid from North Carolina get involved in the sport of rodeo?

My dad was a different kind of cowboy, but he was also the best father I could have ever asked for. My mom bought tickets to rodeos all across the USA, from big rodeos like Cheyenne to the country's smallest, small town rodeos. We went everywhere and anywhere for a rodeo. Dad would grab day sheets (if there even were any) and he, my brother, and I would guess cowboys' scores throughout the rodeo. If Dad guessed the score correctly, I thought he was some sort of PRCA Superhero and if I guessed correctly I'd be a smartass and never let him forget it. If we didn't have a day sheet we'd use Dad's little notebook he just always seemed to have in his pocket. That's just how things rolled. When the PBR came along, Dad and I were in front of the TV for every live broadcast (literally, every single one). We memorized stats, percentages, hometowns, stock contractors, and bull genetics.

Now, I spend my days talking to the guys I grew up watching, talking to the guys my dad respected, and he's not here for that. Dad never got to see my writing career really take off, he always believed that it would, but I just wish he was here to witness it. I wish I could tell my dad that I talked to Fred Whitfield last week or that I have Ty Murray's cell phone number; things that would seemingly be insignificant to so many would've been the things he thought were so cool.

So, if you want to know why I do what I do, why I'm a workaholic, that's why. Because my mom made the reservations, my dad and I kicked the judge's butts at scoring, and my brother tolerated me spouting off countless facts, stats, and scores without pausing to take a breath.

This is for you, Dad. Thank you for being the best father, teacher, and friend I could have ever asked for.

Cimmaron Gerke

Cimmaron Gerke is from Brighton, Colorado. Cimmaron entered the rodeo world at 10 years old; he turned pro at 18. As a student at Odessa College in Odessa, TX, Cimmaron won a College National Title for bareback riding on the school's rodeo team; he went to the NFR the following year.

Cimmaron qualified for 5 National Finals; he won 5 go-rounds and the average at the 2005 NFR. He has won numerous rodeos and is a two-time Cheyenne Frontier Days Champion.

Due to numerous injuries and surgeries, Cimmaron took a step back from rodeo following the 2008 season. He has had 7 surgeries since 2008: shoulder, elbow, both feet, ankle, three ruptured discs in his back, and had his stomach muscles reattached to his pelvis.

In order to rehabilitate his brain and body, Cimmaron has taken up working at Remington Racetrack. He's been breaking, training, and exercising racehorses for over five years and is slowly making his way back into the rodeo arena. Cimmaron has been making his comeback on the PRS (Professional Roughstock Series).

"From Another Planet"

Probably one of my funniest stories is a typical one of a guy down on his luck. The rodeo road is pretty tough and you hit a lot of bumps; luckily, the rough spots can turn into some pretty good situations.

It was right before Cheyenne Frontier Days in 2004. I'd just bought a new rodeo van; it was used, but it ran good. We'd just driven about 6,000 miles in it the week before and it was really holding up. I made the short-go in Cheyenne that week, but before the rodeo I wanted to go to Rock Springs, WY. I'd drawn a horse that I was really itching to get on. My traveling buddy had ditched me for a girl so I figured I'd go by myself. I figured I would be back in time to ride in the short-go at Cheyenne the next day.

I left out that afternoon; it was about 95 degrees out. I get about halfway from Casper to Rawlins, well on my way to Rock Springs and literally in the middle of nowhere, and I blow a tire. I get out, change the tire, and get back on the road as fast as I can so I can make this rodeo.

About 20 minutes later, I blew a second tire. So there I am sitting in the middle of nowhere, no spare, no cell service, and I have a rodeo to get to and another to get back to. I'm literally still sweating from changing the last tire and it's hotter than all get out. I knew some guys would be coming through from Cheyenne along the highway, so I grabbed my gear bag and just started walking down the road.

I got about a mile and a half down the road and these three guys pull up alongside me. "Is that your van back there with the blown tire?" I told them yes and they said, "Well, we usually don't do this, but we'll give you a ride into Rawlins." That sounded great to me so I crawled in and we got to talking.

Turns out they were all geologists and scientists who were out doing research digs and such in Wyoming. They started asking me about rodeo, like what it even was, and as I'm sitting there trying to explain it, I realize they are looking at me like I'm from another planet. They couldn't seem to understand why I did what I did; why I'd voluntarily beat myself up when the paycheck wasn't even guaranteed.

"Why would you get on a bucking horse?"

"Why would you get out of your van and just start walking with your gear bag when it's 97 degrees out?"

I kept trying to explain that I was just determined to get to this rodeo in Rock Springs and I needed to make a living. I kept listening to them talk about the lay of the land and the topographical specs of Wyoming. I was trying to figure out their lifestyle as much as they were trying to figure out mine.

We finally got into Rawlins and I was able to get in touch with a buddy who would stop and pick me up on his way to Rock Springs. We made it to the rodeo just in time and I ended up winning. I won about $700 or $800, which ironically is about what it cost to get my van towed in and have new tires put on it.

But those guys came to the rodeo that night and watched me go; and I just thought that was so cool. I couldn't stay because we had to turn around and drive back to Cheyenne that night. I ended up winning Cheyenne the next day, so it ended up being a really special weekend.

I was just so frustrated with this new van and that my buddy had ditched me for a girl. Then I won two rodeos back to back. It's just a story that'll always stick in the back of my mind. I just can't believe the cards played out like they did and I'll always appreciate those guys giving me a ride.

"Adrenaline Junkies"

Before I ever got involved in rodeo, I was big into dirt bikes. I'd raced some, but sat out for a bit after I got hurt in the fourth grade.

After that, rodeo just took over for the next 10 or 12 years of my life. I didn't think much about dirt bikes or anything but rodeo. College came along and I started thinking it'd be cool and fun to have a street bike. It made more sense then driving all over the place and I really missed having a bike.

So I bought a Kawasaki Ninja, just to ride around on and pretend I was super cool. A late night fight with an ex led to me wrecking that bike into an old lady's car...and then into her house. I ended up in the hospital with a bunch of broken ribs. I had some scrapes and bruises, but overall I was really lucky to be alive. I can't say the same for my bike.

About five years later towards the end of the rodeo year, my buddies and I were up north, I was guaranteed heading to my second NFR. I was having a hell of a good couple of weeks; everything was just clicking and I felt good about everything.

So we're headed to Walla Walla, Washington and on the way there was a really nice Honda CBR for sale on the side of the road. People would call it a "crotch rocket" or whatever. I knew it'd be fast. I told the guys in the van that if I went to Pendleton and won, then I'd come back and buy that bike.

I did go on to win Pendleton, and Spokane the weekend after that. So here I was a young, dumb kid with a lot of money to blow. Forest Bramwell, Michael Moore, Jason Maclean, and myself were supposed to be headed for Albuquerque, but I'd drawn really poorly and didn't want to go. So we went back, I bought the bike, and we headed towards home in Colorado.

Everyone but Jason took turns riding it from Walla Walla to Colorado. They were going to drop me off and keep on for New Mexico from there. Well, right before we got to Forest's house in Pagosa Springs, we noticed the back tire on the bike. It looked like it was going to blow at any second the tire was so bald. We're all standing around scratching our heads about what to do. How were we going to get this bike all the way to my house?

We ended up throwing out the futon bed that was in the back of the van and loaded the bike in its place. Then we all scrunched up in the van for the remaining three hours. After we got to Forest's house I went and got a new tire. I strapped it to my gear bag, and then strapped both of those to bike. I rode over Wolf Creek Pass all the way home to Brighton, CO. Needless to say my parents were not impressed when I pulled in the driveway on a motorcycle.

After all that I guess I can say I rode a motorcycle halfway across the USA. A few years later I ended up wrecking it -my history caught up with me. I sold what was left of it. I don't think any of those guys will forget that bike or those three long hours squished together in the van. I know I won't.

Rand Selle

Rand Selle is a man of many trades: saddle bronc rider, pickup man, leather worker, cowboy poet, and horse trainer. Rand was born in Miles City, Montana to a ranch and rodeo family. Growing up on his family's ranch, Rand learned about the cattle business from his father and bookkeeping from his mom. Rand's two uncles were rodeo cowboys, one rode bareback and the other rode roughstock and roped. Rand chose to follow in his uncles' footsteps instead of going into the cattle business with his father and brother. Rand credits his Uncle Don for his influence on his love of ranch rodeos and being a pickup man.

Rand attended National American University in Rapid City, South Dakota. As a student he interned for Smith Pro Rodeo; learning how to run rodeos, haul stock, and the inner-workings of the business. During his time with Smith Pro Rodeo, Rand had his own opening act riding a bucking bronc in the dark illuminated solely by spotlights and pyrotechnics. When Rand graduated in 2007 he worked as a recruiter for NAU's equine program and rodeo team. When his position was eliminated due to budget cuts, Rand moved back to Miles City, Montana. He worked for Miles Community College recruiting for their rodeo team. Rand and head coach Wally Badgett took a last place team and shot them to third in the region.

In 2009 Rand moved back to Texas where he continued his work for Smith Pro Rodeos when the company obtained Mesquite Pro Rodeo. Rand eventually moved to Dixon, WY to work with Wayne Larsen at Bad Medicine Rodeo. Rand helped put on ranch rodeos, being a pickup man, hauling stock, and investing his mind and wallet in the business of breeding broncs.

To support his passions Rand works in the Wyoming oil and gas fields as a production operator. The job allows him to continue with his love of rodeo by having him "on" for eight days and then six days off, a balance that Rand has taken to with ease.

"Backfired"

When I was with Smith Pro Rodeo I had my own opening act. I'd go out on a bronc and get about 2-3 bucks out of the chute before the pyrotechnics went off. We'd pack these little cannons with about a pound of gunpowder and my buddy would set them off once I was a couple jumps away from the chute. They'd turn into these big ol' flames and silhouette the bronc and I.

One time in Texas we were at this rodeo known for having over the top stunts - the best of the best. I was 20 or 21 and wanted to be the greatest they'd seen. I mean, I was just being driven by my ego at this point.

This grey horse called Cow Camp was a big part of the act. He was just this nice jump and kicker, straight down the arena, real nice and honest. I'm not sure what happened, but one night he set up right in front of the chute and was just swooping back and forth. The pyrotechnic guy couldn't tell I hadn't gotten away from the chutes before he set the flames off. We were so close that it singed the hair off the back of my neck and set Cow Camp's tail on fire.

So I'm spurring this bronc, and I smell burning hair and I can't tell if it's mine or his or what is going on. I have some pictures of it, and you can see his tail just a smokin'. The heat was insane; the back of my hat was a little black and uh, crisp.

Another time in Rapid City, South Dakota we had some wild colt that we'd never used before. We'd only had enough room on the trailer for the broncs so we didn't have my normal set-up.

So I ended up getting on these outlawed, wild suckers, and it was all I could do to stay on when those flames went off. They'd have strobe lights going in front of the bucking chutes, and those colts would take about one jump out of the chutes, see those lights, and absolutely flip out. Here I am trying to look super cool, like I'm in control, while I wasn't even remotely sure I was going to walk out of the arena.

Probably one of the wilder trips I've had was in Jackson, Mississippi. They have 10 performances in seven days down there. I had also entered so I ended up getting on 11 horses in seven days. I know that the guys at the NFR have it rough 'cause 11 head in seven days beat me up pretty good.

About the 4th or 5th performance I had to get on the "rank stock" that really bucked. There was this mare Bandera Gold, and she literally exploded out the chute. I made it about three jumps on her, then she saw those strobe lights. She ducked and dodged left, and bucked me off so hard I was almost knocked out. This "Wildest Bronc Ride" is going on and she is just beating the hell out of me.

She ended up breaking the buckle off my belt; like completely unsnapped it and sent it flying. I had a watch on. That broke too, and I lost my hat. I had this little wallet I'd carry with like my driver's license and credit cards. I don't know how she did it, but she worked that out of my pocket and not only sent it flying, but all my cards too.

So my driver's license and credit cards are strewn all over the arena floor, when the lights finally came back on. My buddy is out there scrounging around in the dirt trying to get my stuff together and I couldn't even catch my air to go help him.

Those days the opening act were pretty wild and wooly. I got on some great horses and the act was really popular. I'm not sure the crowd knew exactly how wild things were getting down on the arena floor.

"Moustache Ask You To Dance"

I'm sure I'll catch grief all over again for this, but it's a pretty good joke on me.

I'd just moved to Texas. I had only been there a few weeks when a bunch of us took off for "winter run" and ended up in Lafayette, LA.

Everybody is all pumped up about me doing my opening act for the first time. We run through it a couple times, everything goes great; we're ready to roll. We thought it was going to be big and people were going to love it. Harper Morgan Rodeo Company was really well known for these big, top of the line acts, so I was stoked. They'd have timed shootouts, long horned steers running around, black lights- just really ahead of their game for the times so it was a big deal for me.

That night after the rodeo everyone headed to this bar, a pretty famous "after party" place. I think it was called Cowboys. Everyone was shaking my hand, telling me how cool it was, and I just thought I was awesome. I was so pumped up, just on Cloud 9. I thought I was the top dog, the king, and my 21-year-old ego was bursting at the seams. All the guys were chiding me with, "Come on and go to the bar with us!" I said, "Yeah, sure! That sounds great!" I figured there would be dancing and I'd just soak it up and enjoy the ego trip I was on.

So we get to the bar and this announcer Andy Stewart is introducing me right and left and talking me up. He's this big ol' dude with a massive moustache so everyone knows him. The bar is filled with people. It's loud and crazy. They were going to do topless bull riding after midnight; so we think we're in for just a hell of a night. I get a couple drinks in me and I am feeling really good, like really good.

This really pretty girl shows up, and it so happens her brother Kenny is a bullfighter. He sees me taking notice of her, and says, "Take my sister out on the dance floor and spin her around." I'm out there dancing around, having a good time, just enjoying life.

Well, I come back and all of a sudden all of the guys are looking at me weird and I'm like, "No biggie." I just shook it off and figured it wasn't a big deal. I go to the restroom and come back. I'm standing with this group of guys again and everyone is kind of giving me a dirty look. I was like, "Hey Kenny, can I dance with your sister again?" He goes on about how he doesn't think she's into me anymore. I was like, "Well, why? What's wrong?" and Kenny goes, "Well she's not into gay guys." I was like, "What the hell are you talking about? I'm as straight as they come. Kenny, come on man, I love women."

So Kenny's going on and on about how they don't do that kind of stuff and my mind is just spinning. I can't figure out what's going on and I'm a little intoxicated. I notice that this big announcer dude is standing next to me. "Kenny, why? What's wrong?" and Kenny goes, "Well, Andy the announcer just told us you're gay!"

"DO WHAT!" So I whipped my head around to confront this guy, and this sucker grabs me by the head and lays a massive moustache-filled kiss right on my mouth! All I could feel was his moustache on my face.

Needless to say, it turned out to be a bit of a "hazing" but man, I puked everywhere. I was so mad I took off back to the rodeo grounds, which was not in the best part of town and pretty far off. I was just so mad! Looking back now I can laugh and think it's funny, but at the time I was so embarrassed.

They'd just decided to humble me a bit and bring me back down to earth. It was my "introduction" to the group so to speak; they just embarrass the shit out of you. Of course now it's this ongoing joke and we're such a family we pick on each other about everything, but that first one was a little rough.

"Hog Wild"

One day at the ranch we had to go out and round up these bulls. It was just nasty trees and brush, really rough riding, you can't hardly ride through it. It took us three days to get these suckers spotted. The first two days we managed to get one or two roped before it got too hot, then we'd go back in the evening and try again.

One day a couple of the PRCA judges came along to round up these bulls. They were in between rodeos and came to the ranch to hang out. We had work to do, so we just saddled up a couple horses for them and brought them along. We're headed into these trees and I get my grey horse locked onto this bull; I mean we're running WIDE OPEN trying to get close enough to rope him. It was like this bull had a target on him and my horse was aimed for it, totally focused.

These judges are behind me, trying to keep up and keep me in sight. All of a sudden a bunch of wild hogs come flying out of the brush, almost run underneath their horses and their horses just freaked out. These horses took off and these judges are getting completely run away with.

Suddenly I don't see them anymore. I get this bull roped out in this opening and I'm waiting for someone to come along and help me out. All of a sudden, through the trees, I spot one of the judges, and his horse is still taking off with him- after a solid 20 minutes! I'm just sitting there and watching the shit hit the fan. I mean I couldn't go help them or anything because I have this bull on the other end of my rope.

Finally someone saw me sitting out in the open and came out to help me. Those judges finally got back to the trailers, but they could not get those horses to go back in the trees anymore. They just stuck to riding out in the open spots. It never did bother my grey horse, but those other horses were scarred for life.

Cole Elshere

Cole Elshere is a saddle bronc rider from Faith, South Dakota. Cole began riding when he was 11, climbing aboard two bareback horses after watching his cousins ride. When Cole was 13 he climbed aboard his first saddle bronc horse.

Cole continued to ride at every level growing up, even throughout his time at Gillette College. Cole turned pro after college. He's qualified for three National Finals (2012, 2013, 2014). Cole placed in Round 2 and 3 at the 2014 National Finals.

In Spring 2014 Cole signed on to play legendary South Dakota rodeo man Casey Tibbs in an upcoming documentary "Floating Horses" that will begin filming in May of 2015.

When he's not on the road, Cole is helping work cattle on his family's ranch in South Dakota.

"Hello, Hollywood Calling"

I was out feeding cows when I got the call about being in the Casey Tibbs movie; to be honest, they kind of caught me off guard. We talked for an hour or so about what my part would entail, filming, etc. They didn't have a script for me to read, they had just called me up to see if I was interested in playing the part. Both sides decided that I fit the part, and I really wanted to play Casey, so we went with it.

Every aspect of it is really cool, between it being a big production deal and that Casey was from my home state. There's tons of saddle bronc history in it too, which clearly matters to me. It's just such an honor to be able to play one of my heroes and help keep his legacy alive.

We're going to be filming the bronc riding scenes in Ft. Pierre, South Dakota and the fact that it's centered in South Dakota is awesome. There is a lot of history with it that people aren't aware of, and I'm glad I get to be a part of it. Casey Tibbs was so influential to so many and now I get to help carry his name forward.

"Jitters"

The first time I ever qualified for the National Finals I probably wasn't as nervous as I should have been.

You know, we get there a couple days early to practice the Grand Entry and do a lot of media. Every time we rode out into the arena you get psyched up, really going. Whether it's climbing down into the chutes and getting settled or riding out in the middle of that arena, it's the best feeling in the world.

But man, when I climbed in the chute onto my first horse, it just washed over me, "Oh boy, here we go…" There's a lot of good pressure and there's a lot of bad pressure too. I finally felt the nerves starting to kick in a bit.

Thomas & Mack has these big, high-energy crowds, and that's the best kind of rodeo you can get. I love rodeos where the crowd's energy fills the whole arena. Just sitting in the chute you can feel the electricity in the atmosphere. That feeling was definitely feeding my nerves as well.

My first out I was on this pretty young horse that no one really knew about. The unknown aspect made me a bit nervous, but I was just trying to look at it like any other ride. I had no idea what to expect and just thought, "Here I am at the NFR for the first time!" I just tried to downplay the nerves. I just didn't want to get bucked off. Between the young horse and the crowd my nerves were jumpy at best.

My travel buddies had come down for the bronc futurity, so that was good to have them there. Chad Ferley, fellow South Dakotan and bronc rider, was with me too. He'd been showing me the ropes since my 1st time around, which I really appreciated. I've always looked up to him and asked him for advice and I didn't want to let him down. A ton of family and friends came and hung out which was so helpful; I just didn't want to disappoint them. They'd come all this way and I wanted to ride my best and make them proud.

That year I ended up finishing 4th at the NFR and 7th in the world.

My 2nd trip to the NFR was in 2013. Mentally, I felt more confident than the previous year. I'd "been there, done that" and done really well in 2012. I felt the pressure a little more and the nerves a little less. My mindset had become, "Okay, now it's time to get to business." A lot of guys don't make it back the second year so that was really my goal, to get back there and ride just as well as I had in 2012. Chad Ferley had traveled back to Vegas with me and he was just as much help as ever. He actually went on to be the World Champion that year.

Overall, I just let the pressure get to me and didn't perform as well as I'd have liked to. I finished 11th in the world after Finals and I should've been in the Top 10, no problem. Now I'm focused on making it back in 2014 and really learning from my past experiences.

At this level you're just shooting for first place, no matter what, and second place just never satisfies you. You want to win. It's just a different feeling when you get the chance to be first. It's way more rewarding when you're able to achieve that.

"Humble Beginnings"

When I'm not on the road I always head home to my family's ranch in South Dakota. I pitch in and help whether it's fixing fences or moving stock, I'm there to lend a hand with the workload.

Ranch life is just as rewarding as rodeo, in my opinion, but in a very different way. I always enjoy going home and it always helps me. When I head back out on the road I have a fresh perspective about things. Just being home and being able to do something successfully, even if it's just tamping a post, it just gets you ramped back up and ready to go. Those little victories help keep you humble for sure.

After the NFR in 2012, I'd had a really good NFR, I headed home until the season picked back up again. It'd been a few days since the bright lights of Las Vegas and things were back to work as usual.

We'd gone out to trail cows from our south place to where we were going to calve them in the spring months. It wasn't a long trail, maybe 5 miles at most, but it was snowing sideways and the wind was blowing right through my clothes.

So here I was freezing to death on this horse in the middle of South Dakota and just a couple of days earlier I'd been sitting in Las Vegas with a t-shirt on riding high on my first National Finals performance.

Times like that just prove to me that you always have to stay humble because something will always bring you back to reality. You can be chasing gold buckles one day, but reality always comes knocking. Rodeo and ranch life both give me something; they are both equally as rewarding.

Matthew Bohman

Matthew Bohman has made his living training horses since he was sixteen years old. His primary focus is young and challenging horses.

After working with and learning from several well-known and respected trainers and horsemen about cutting, cow horses, roping and reining, Matthew was presented with a career-changing decision.

After much soul-searching he decided to take his experience and years of training problematic and fresh horses to a different level. Matthew started 2-year-olds for NRHA Hall of Famer, Bob Loomis in Overbrook, Oklahoma. He then moved Weatherford, TX and worked for Matt Gaines.

Matthew's willingness to share his experience and knowledge with those who are serious about improving their horsemanship is the driving force behind his new clinic program. He is now available for clinics and lessons as well as a limited number of colt starts and training.

"Great Horses"

There are three horses that always stick in my mind, Dove, Ace, and Levi.

I'm originally from Ohio and I was going to a Branch Campus for college. I had a barn up there and was training while I was going to school. While teaching a clinic in Dayton, OH, I told people that I was going to have to find a better way to keep my horses up there. This lady JoAnn asked, "Why don't you just move in with my husband and me?" It caught me off-guard that people could be that nice. It wasn't long before I took her up on her offer and I moved in with them.

I was living just south of the city and helping them out with their barn and horses. She had this horse Dove, by an Andalusian stallion and Percheron mare, so naturally just a really hot horse. JoAnn's friend had this other horse, Ace, out of the same stallion and Thoroughbred mare. This lady's sister had rescued, so to speak, the third horse, Levi. So here I am with three super hot-blooded horses.

These ladies had started to have issues with their horses. The horses were really smart but just "on point" all the time. Dove wasn't too hard to figure out; she was just hot and fractious. Some dressage trainers had just tried to jerk her around in all these big bits and I ended up having my best success on her in a hackamore.

I learned a lot from Dove about how there are other options and other ways to approach things. Even just a snaffle bit didn't set right with her. People think hackamores are for more experienced, well-trained horses, but Dove just took to it almost instantly. At that point I realized that for her, at that point in her training, a hackamore was going to be my best option.

Ace was a massive gelding and his owner was this tiny lady who was used to riding Arabians. Suddenly she had this huge, hot horse and she didn't know what to do with him. She was used to Arabs jumping around and being flighty, but they're pretty light and dainty and she'd grown used to that. Ace was just a powerhouse in the saddle and on the ground; he just had to learn about respect.

Of all these horses I probably learned the most from Levi. He was definitely the trickiest. He was previously owned by an older lady, who tried to teach him to drive before she taught him anything else. She'd gone about it in a really poor way. I'd found out she'd tied her husband's flight suit to him to help desensitize him. You know, the kind of suit pilots wear. It'd make a bunch of noise in the wind so she thought if he just packed it around he'd get used to it, which clearly was not the case.

Levi ended up being terrified of everything. His situation was bad enough that JoAnn's friend rescued him. He wasn't neglected or anything; he just wasn't working out for the older lady.

The first day I worked with Levi I had to rope him just to catch him. He was a very intelligent horse. He'd just stand there with haunches cocked towards you and wait. You could get about five feet from him and he'd just walk off. He wouldn't run away or turn on you; he'd just walk away. He had learned that this was a fantastic game and a way to get out of work.

After I roped him and got a halter on him he wasn't too bad. We just did some groundwork initially and he didn't seem to be phased. I went to get on him and as soon as some weight hit that stirrup, he came unglued. He was a little over 16 hands and about 1250lbs, and I just went flying backwards. I decided that we'd better just stick to groundwork for a while until I figured out all of his buttons.

I worked with him for about a week and thought I kind of had him figured out. I'd rope him off of Dove every day and he was getting used to her being in the round pen with us. By the end of the week I could ride him around without any major issues. His owner wanted to come see him and I figured we'd progressed enough that I could show her what all we'd accomplished.

I climbed on him and we'd walked, trotted, and loped around the arena. He was just being perfect. She was really excited, and then as I'm standing there just talking to her, he melted down. I felt like I did five summersaults off the back of him, got the wind knocked out of me and bashed in my shoulder pretty good.

Of course his owner has witnessed all this and she was absolutely white-knuckled grabbing the round pen fence. She's going, "I am never riding that horse!" I talked to her for a bit and convinced her to let me keep working with him. In the moment he bucked me off I realized he had a really uneducated mouth. It wasn't that he was lacking knowledge, but that he was just dull to my hand. He didn't understand what he was being asked to do and so he'd panic.

I went back to the basics and I ground drove him all over the arena. I might have been able to do it on his back, but other people needed to be able to handle him as well. So I'd line drive him until he'd soften up and was responsive to my hand and then do some groundwork. Flagging him out every day and then and I'd pony him off Dove regularly.

As soon as he learned to respect his halter and the lightness of my hands in the bridle I felt more comfortable riding him. It took me at least another week before I could swing a leg over and start riding him a without him coming unhinged. The first day I climbed back on him I had just done about an hour of groundwork and ridden him for about 10 minutes. Three weeks later, it was 20 minutes of groundwork and 40 minutes in the saddle. It was a really slow progression. That's what it needed to be. He'd been rushed before and that's when he'd panic.

The second time I climbed on I didn't even ask him to move his feet, the next day I did the same thing. I wanted him to stand there quietly and know that he was going to be fine. The third and fourth day we just walked, then the fifth and sixth we trotted a bit, etc. After about two weeks we could walk, trot, and lope without him attempting to buck.

I decided his owner needed to come back out and see how much progress he'd made; that he wasn't attempting to buck me off anymore and didn't feel the need to panic. So Cathy came over to see Levi. At that time he was still a bit difficult to catch so we just went out in the pasture. We were just standing there talking about horses and the work I'd been doing. She was telling me how she was going to sell him or give him away because she just couldn't do anything with him.

Unbeknownst to Cathy, here comes Levi ambling up behind her and he nudged her with his nose. She absolutely freaked out, initially because it scared her and then because she couldn't believe he'd just walked up to us out there in the pasture. A month earlier he didn't want anything to do with people and here he was nuzzling her for some attention.

Cathy left him in training with me for another month. At the end of that month she came over in hopes of riding him. She put on her helmet, and I could see how nervous she was. She slowly climbed up and off they went. Levi walked, trotted, and loped around like it was any other day. A month earlier I'd seen this lady absolutely terrified of her horse and now she's riding him around like it was second nature to both of them.

It was just an extremely rewarding feeling for me to see both of them overcome such states of fear and panic to comfortably work together. I think about that horse a lot; I've learned so much since then and I wish I could go back and apply it. If I knew then what I know now, I could have done some amazing things with him. He went on to have a very successful career in the dressage arena and I'm happy with that.

Those three were my first real experiences with problem horses; at least working on them by myself without a mentor there and figuring things out on my own. It made me far more confident about what I was doing and who I wanted to be and it was equally rewarding for me as it was for the horse and the owner. It made me more confident in my program and my approach to horses. There's lots of different ways you can go about things by taking your time and realizing what past history is affecting your current ride; it makes a difference.

"Big Engine"

I was in Texas working for Bruce Logan and there was an eight-year old black Egyptian gelding. His name was Diesel because when he'd snort he sounded like an old diesel engine turning over. He was huge, big and lanky with these jet black eyes and polished coat.

This horse had endurance in his blood; he was bred to lope across the desert and he was flighty on top of that. He was eight years old, had

8 different owners so far, and had never been successfully ridden. Apparently Diesel was great until he got a saddle on him. People would tack him up and watch him go to bucking and just call it quits. He was really strong and endurance wise he'd just buck and buck….and buck.

Diesel finally ended up coming to us when his owner declared us her last resort. Well, we took Diesel out into the big arena, saddled him up, and he went to bucking just like everyone said. He was throwing himself into the side of the round pen, just being overly dramatic. That kept up for a solid ten minutes; for a horse to buck that hard and for that long was almost incomprehensible. It took ten minutes just for him to slow down and eventually stop.

He stood there long enough to catch his breath and then went right back to it. We left him at it and for about three hours he just bucked as hard as he could. He'd stop and catch his breath and go at it again. The next day he did the same thing, only not throwing himself into the sides of the round pen. It was another day of solid, full-force bucking.

It took us two weeks before we could put a saddle on him and he'd just stand there. He knew that bucking his brains out wasn't going to get the saddle off. He'd had terrible experiences in the past, but he'd learned that if he bucked then the saddle came off and he didn't have to work. He finally got to where he'd stop bucking and come over to the side of the round pen to greet people. He was just looking for someone to save him from that saddle. As soon as you walked away he'd go right back to it.

This was my first real ranch job, and after about a month of another guy riding Diesel, Bruce decided it was my turn. Over breakfast Bruce just plainly said, "Well, Matthew, I think it's your turn to ride Diesel." I literally felt the blood drain from my face; I didn't think he meant so soon. I wasn't sure if I was ready or if Bruce even thought I was ready.

I knew it was time for Diesel to start handling multiple riders and people. I just didn't know that I was going to be the second contestant. I was definitely worried as I stepped up on him. I knew if he started bucking it wasn't going to be pretty. We ponied him around and he didn't buck or anything, but he was always just kind of flighty. It was a huge confidence booster for me though, that he didn't even attempt to buck and for as nervous as I was he didn't feed off that too much.

We finally got him to where he was fine to go out on the range and we could rope calves off of him. One day we were out gathering cows in prickly pears and mesquite; it was rough territory. We came across an old barbed-wire fence that was half torn down, kind of spooky. Diesel rocked back and just launched over this fence, he had so much self-preservation he wasn't even going to put himself in the position to get caught up in the barbed wire.

He caught me off guard though and it pitched me to the left, which scared him. He bolted off and we ended up on this old oil road. My right hand was on the horn, my left hand was in his mane trying to hold on, my right spur was luckily up in the saddle versus being dug in his side, and I was just trying to work my way back up into the middle of him. I didn't have a chance to grab the reins or anything; he was just galloping along at his own free will. I finally got myself pulled back up in the middle and the second my butt hit the saddle he settled back into a trot and eventually stopped.

Another time we were gathering cows and my boss didn't have the gate open far enough. My foot got caught in the gate and Diesel just kept on walking forward. As I slowly peeled off the saddle and hit the dirt, here goes Diesel bucking down the dirt road. He bucked this big old circle, came back up to me and looked at me like, "Why did you come off of me? That scared me." I just climbed back on like nothing had happened. He never thought about bucking after that.

For all the bucking we saw him do, how long and how hard he'd buck, he'd never been ridden by anybody for longer than maybe five minutes before he came to us. It's not that he was cold-backed or anything, he was just flighty. That horse just taught me so much about sitting in the middle of a horse, using my seat, and the psychology of a horse and how much they need a leader. The more leadership I gave him, the more confident he was, which I've learned is the case with any horse.

Jace Angus

Jace Angus hails from Fallon, Nevada. Jace's ranch and rodeo roots go back generations. His great-grandfather competed at Cheyenne Frontier Days in the 1920's and his maternal grandfather drove a chuckwagon throughout the Depression. At 22 Jace graduated from McNeese State University with a degree in Kinesiology and then Jace went on to obtain his PRCA card that same year.

In 2014 Jace got an offer to train cow horses in New York. Jace is sponsored by Lost Cowboy, an apparel company that supports the cowboy way and traditional America.

When he's not on the road with rodeo, Jace spends his spare time training horses, working racehorses, and learning how to surf.

"Legacy"

My grandfather has always been one of my heroes. He drove a chuckwagon throughout the Depression and was a true ranchman. In May 2014 I drew a horse in Auburn, CA that I had also drawn back at Cow Palace the previous fall. I'd had a good ride on him then, but he just hadn't been enough horse to win the rodeo on.

My whole family, including my grandfather, had come to Auburn to see me ride. He wasn't very strong anymore but he'd come to watch me compete. My dad was a bronc rider too, so he was back behind the chutes with me. My mom sat in the stands with my grandfather.

I always love having my family come to rodeos. My dad is always talking shit with me and if I buck off he's laughing at me as I'm walking back. He's really encouraging just before I go but he always has to crack the jokes and give me a hard time, you know, "Don't be a sissy! Go be a cowboy!"

Going into Auburn I felt confident because I knew what to expect. I figured if the little horse bucked a little harder and I rode him just as well I'd be up there in the money. Well, I ended up winning my first pro rodeo with my grandfather sitting in the stands watching.

After my ride I found my grandfather. He stood up, shook my hand and said, "Hell of a bronc ride, Jace."

He passed away two weeks after that.

It meant so much to me that he was there and my mom and dad too. It was my first pro rodeo win and to have them there just made it all the more meaningful to me.

Chad Eubank

Chad Eubank, a Cleburne, Texas native, made a name for himself during his time at Hill College where he earned the title of 2003 National Intercollegiate Rodeo Association World Champion Bull Rider. In 2003, he was also named the NIRA Southern Region Champion All-Around Cowboy, Champion Bull Rider and Champion Bareback Rider.

Chad was able to showcase his rodeo talent on Spike TV's Toughest Cowboy series as one of only four competitors that competed in 2007, 2008, and 2009 in bull riding, saddle bronc, and bareback riding.

Chad decided to take his passion on the road where he won major rodeos including Cheyenne Frontier Days, Fort Worth Stock Show and Rodeo, and Barretos Brazil International Rodeo. He finished in the Top 20 roughstock riders in the world, in the Top 15 All Around Cowboys in the world, and set the arena record at the Pikes Peak or Bust Rodeo Colorado Sprints Short-go where he was crowned the champion.

After he retired from the rodeo circuit, he decided to use his horsemanship skills and began training cutting, reining, roping and working cow horses. Chad is a member of APHA, NCHA, AQHA, NRHA, SHOT, and PTHA.

Chad actively participates and sits on the Board of Directors at the Children's Advocacy Center in Cleburne, Texas. He has a real heart for the mission of restoring hope in the lives of children that have suffered abuse.

Chad currently lives and trains at Chad Eubank Performance Horses, located between Keene and Egan, Texas with his two children and wife Nikki.

"Taking A Redeye"

In 2003, I was 21 and had just bought my own place in Hillsboro, Texas. I went to Tarleton State and flunked out. So I bought my own place and started training horses and going to rodeo. Paul Brown, the rodeo coach for Hill College, knew I still had eligibility left when it came to college rodeo, so he found out where I lived.

He kept pestering me to go back to school. I was making my own way in life and just didn't want to go back. Well, he must have worn me down because I finally decided to go back and join the rodeo team.

The team ended up going to the College National Finals that year. I won the region in bareback riding, bull riding, and the All-Around. I was second in the saddle bronc. So off we went to the CNFR. At the CNFR I was the only cowboy in history to score above an 80-point score on all four bulls and the only bull rider in history to win all four rounds.

While I was at the CNFR there was a bull named L72-Redeyes. I saw this bull and wanted nothing to do with him; he was just that bad. I was super glad I hadn't drawn him while I was there.

Later that year, I was living in Montrose, Colorado and training futurity barrel horses for the TJ Bar Ranch. My buddies and I would go up to Steamboat Springs every few weeks for the rodeo. They have this little pro rodeo series all summer long. One weekend we'd entered up and I drew this bull, L72-Redeyes.

I didn't even realize who he was until I went to put my rope on him. The bull riding comes up and they run him up in the chutes and as I'm putting my rope on him and realize what I'm dealing with. I wasn't scared of him, just tried to look at him like he was any other bull. Looking back, if I'd dwelled on it too much I would've psyched myself out, no question. I ended up being 88 on him and it was the first time he'd ever had a qualified ride.

A couple years later I was at Pikes Peak or Bust and they offered me a re-ride, which I took; and the re-ride was ol' L72-Redeyes. I took the re-ride knowing how things had been previously. I ended up being 91 on him and set the arena record at the indoor coliseum.

In 2007 I was at Cheyenne Frontier Days. I called to get my draw and my 2nd round bull just happened to be L72-Redeyes. So far, I was the only guy to have ridden him twice and here I was drawing him a third time. I was 91 on him at CFD and ended up winning the All-Around that year. I was the first roughstock rider in 10 years to win the All-Around at Cheyenne and it was because of that bull.

We really fit each other like a glove, his moves matched my moves and it just clicked. His style is really wild and unorthodox, and I just really enjoyed it. I never really liked riding bulls; I just did it because I could and financially it was pretty good to me. I always preferred bucking horses to bulls, but with the combination they made me a living.

So, this bull that initially I hadn't wanted anything to do with ended up painting my career a little bit more glorious than it would've been. He'll always be one of my favorite bulls. My 3-year-old son runs around wearing an All-Around buckle from the Daddy of 'Em All thanks to Ol' Redeyes.

Timmy Shanahan

Timmy Shanahan, from Flemington, New Jersey has been riding for 4 years, obtaining his PRCA permit in 2013. He credits the decision to become a rodeo man to his older sister Katie. At age four Timmy walked into his family's living room to see his sister watching Professional Bull Riders (PBR) on TV, and he was hooked, "From that moment on I wanted to be a rodeo cowboy."

In 2010 Timmy climbed aboard his first bull at a local ranch that had some practice bulls available and was giving him the opportunity to ride. "They gave me about a 5-minute briefing on what to do and then I took my wrap."

When Timmy graduated high school in 2011 he turned down multiple colligate track and field scholarships, instead deciding to pursue his passion for rodeo. When he's not on the road with his traveling partner Eric Tomasello, Timmy can be found volunteering for the local fire department, kayaking, fishing, and spending as much time outside as possible.

Timmy was a qualifier in the bareback riding at the 2013 and 2014 First Frontier Circuit Finals.

Timmy is currently the farm manager at White Pole Stables, LLC. in Pittstown, NJ.

"Put Your Left Hand In"

Two weeks after I got on my first bull, I competed in my first rodeo. I drew a bull named White Trash. He was a big, white bull and other than that, I knew absolutely nothing about him. That didn't matter though, nothing mattered. I was about to make my childhood dream a reality. I had all the confidence in the world that night.

Since it was a local rodeo, my friends and family showed up; siblings, cousins and even the grandparents came out for the Saturday evening showdown. I was sitting on the top rail of the chute gate when the bullfighter pointed to me and said, "Get ready."

Without hesitation I dropped my left foot down onto the back of White Trash; and instantly he threw his head back and slung snot into the air covering my vest. It didn't phase me; I was a cowboy. I gently knelt on his back, sliding my legs on either side of him, keeping my boots on the slats. I handed my tail up to Chris Tejero, the "Cancun Kid" himself. He had been letting me get on his bulls at home and he knew I wanted this. He pulled it tight enough for me to heat up my rosin, just like I had been taught a few weeks earlier. Tapping my tail with the back of my hand, I gave the signal I was done heating up.

Chris gave me some slack as he allowed me to set my handle where I want it, "Pinky on his spine," I thought to myself. "I got this." By this point my heart's racing and butterflies have come on, almost as if there were hundreds of them in my stomach.

To say I was nervous would be accurate. I had no fear of getting hung up, stepped on, or hurt; I was nervous about bucking off. I just wanted to ride. I wanted to be a cowboy.

The Cancun Kid started pulling my rope; nice and easy to make sure it was right. I took my tail and wrapped my hand and I was ready to ride! As I slid up on my hand, White Trash laid down in the chute. Now I had only been on four or five bulls prior to this rodeo, and I was clueless as to what I should do in that kind of situation.

Then I hear from somewhere in the back pens, "Take him; be a cowboy!" It was all the motivation I needed. I nodded my head and ol' White Trash came blowing out of that chute like a jack-in-the-box. He made three jumps to the right and cracked back to the left. The only thing he did wrong was forgot me... as he spun round and left me lying in the dirt.

In all the commotion he landed on my right hand, breaking it in two places. It was nothing more than a battle scar to be proud of, and turns out, the first of many.

"Wrong Side of The Table"

A couple days before my 19th birthday in 2012, I bought my Professional Bull Riders Permit and headed down to Hampton, VA for a PBR Touring Pro event.

Before the event these tables were set up in the arena for autographs and pictures with the PBR guys. This was my first time doing anything PBR related. I'd only watched the PBR on TV. I was absolutely in awe to be sitting at that table signing autographs.

While the signing was going on, I looked to see Travis Briscoe to my left and Colby Yates to my right. I'd watched these guys ride on TV and here I was sitting next to them signing autographs!

My dad was over by the fence and told him, "Dad, I don't want to be sitting at the table signing autographs. I want to be standing in front of the table getting these guys autographs!" It was a totally surreal moment for me to be next to guys I'd been looking up to for so long.

Colby Yates actually pulled my bull rope that night. I recall asking him if the butterflies ever go away over the years. He'd just chuckled and said, "No, they stick with you." I thought it was really cool he'd even agreed to pull my rope. I totally got bucked off right in front of him and as I climbed back on the chute he patted me on the back. I was little embarrassed I'd bucked off in front of one of my heroes, but it was still a great time.

"All Fun And Games"

Every now and then a rodeo story comes along that really wasn't about the ride or the wreck, but rather it was about the great time before and after the ride. This is one of those stories.

Two years ago my traveling partner Eric Tomasello and I were heading to a rodeo. He was 16 and I was 19. This was going to be his first big rodeo weekend. We were driving down to McHenry, Maryland to a two-night bull riding event.

I picked him up on Friday morning and his mom was clearly pretty nervous about him going. I promised her I'd take care of him and off we went. Arriving in McHenry in the late afternoon, we had a few hours to kill before the rodeo. We did the responsible thing and checked into our hotel and then grabbed a bite to eat. I'll admit, we both felt like big shots walking around with our boots, hats, and shirts. Everywhere we went people would stop and talk to us.

Around 5:30pm we hopped in my truck and headed down the road to the fairgrounds. Now, I don't know how it all started, but I guess when you are a couple of teenagers far from home you have a certain sense of invincibility. In addition, the fact we had been throwing back energy drinks all day and we each had to face a 2,000 pound opponent that night added to the feeling. Overall, it is a recipe for a great time!

Rolling into the fairgrounds we had the windows down and the music cranked up. The latter didn't really matter since you couldn't hear the lyrics over Eric's freestyle rap to Eminem. We were feeling good.

We both rode pretty badly the first night, only making it back to the short-go due to sheer luck and the fact we actually showed up. The night was still young however and we had no intentions of just going back to the hotel and crashing.

It was about 11pm after the rodeo and there was NOTHING to do in McHenry, Maryland except go party at the bars on the lake. That presented one problem: our age. So we did the next best thing and hit up the arcade and go-kart track until 3am!

We were sitting there on racing motorcycles and I was like, "Dude, I just want to point out the fact that we're 3 states away and 6.5 hours from home. Our parents have no clue what we're doing. All they know is we're at a rodeo, and here we are playing arcade games."

Our parents probably thought we were out trying to pick up girls or getting into trouble with the older guys; instead we're the only guys in this massive arcade room just having a blast. We still talk about what an awesome weekend that turned out to be and the beating we both took the next night.

I drew a Mexican fighting bull and had no hope. My two legs would beat his four to the fence, and I took a mighty good hooking. Eric's draw of a big ol' brindle ended up squishing Eric's helmet and face when he landed on him. Eric sprang up and ran straight into the fence; he didn't even make the slightest attempt to jump up on the fence and away from that bull.

I love that kid; we've been traveling partners ever since.

"Easy Breezy"

Probably my favorite bucking horse was Breezy. Her brand was 916 from Cowtown. She was the first horse I ever won money on in the PRCA. In the summer of 2013 I'd taken home a 2nd place check thanks to her.

In April 2014 we met up again in a practice pen and she ended up breaking my leg. I got hung up and drug and she wound up landing on me.

In July 2014 I entered my first PRCA rodeo of the season, just coming back from a broken leg, and dumb luck would have it I drew Breezy again. Everyone told me I should turn out, but that isn't who I am.

I am a cowboy and it was time to show Breezy who was boss. I was so excited to get back on her. She is one of the best horses to ride; she jumps high, kicks hard, and you can fall back and just have fun on her.

There was only one other bareback rider that night, and after he bucked off I knew this was my chance to win it. Settling down onto this mare's flat, wide back I knew I'd won it already. Cracking my bind I was ready. With a nod of my head the gate flew open and Breezy jumped out.

She threw three lightning quick kicks and it all seemed to happen in slow motion; it seemed like she was floating in the air. I just laid back and enjoyed every second of the ride. She darted to the right and then started running moments after the buzzer sounded. She knew I won this time and she was done working for the night.

With a score of 66 and a first place check I was happy for a guy who had been on crutches just two weeks earlier. Hopefully, the next time we meet up she doesn't decide to break me again. That night was a really good night for some redemption, though.

Clay McCuistion

Clay McCuistion is a tie down roper who hails from Sanger, Texas. Clay graduated from Tarleton State University in 2011 with a degree in Agricultural Services and Development.

When Clay is not on the road with rodeo he's investing in his concrete company, his pride and joy. In his free time Clay likes to play the occasional game of golf, spend time with his family and friends, and brainstorm ways to make his business grow.

Clay travels with two horses; his older, reliable horse and a young horse that will be ready to go full-time by the 2015 season.

"CFD"

The summer 2014 I'd been going to amateur rodeos in Texas versus traveling around, and things weren't really going too well. I was getting pretty frustrated and just couldn't seem to get things rolling in the right direction.

My girlfriend, mom, and dad all talked me into going up to Cheyenne Frontier Days and some other rodeos around there. Basically, get out of Texas, go to some different rodeos, and see if things would turn around.

I ended up 7th in the first round at Cheyenne and two spots from placing in the second round. I came back in the short round 6th and ended up winning $6,400. It was a lot more than I ever made at amateur rodeos in Texas, even winning them wouldn't have brought me that kind of money. My mom, dad, grandmother, and girlfriend were all there too, so that was pretty special. Having their support just makes such a difference.

I figured where my roping was at and what I needed to work on. I knew I needed to really figure things out before the 2015 season so I could try to make the National Finals.

It was the first time I'd been on the road for a really significant period of time and professionally I was roping against the best guys in the world. Going into that 2nd round of slack, the crowd got really loud when I tied the calf and it just meant a lot to me. I was leading the average and I roped him in 13.8. It was just a huge confidence boost when I needed one.

I rope left-handed and there have been people who have told me a left-handed roper will never make it to the NFR. I feel like I have the confidence now, that it doesn't matter where I'm at or who I'm roping against. I know I'm capable of winning first place.

"Fore!"

When I was at Cheyenne Frontier Days, Shane Hanchey, Hunter Herrin, and I decided to play a round of golf.

I played a ton in high school and when I graduated I figured there's a lot of people that play golf, and a lot of people that play golf really well. There are not as many people in rodeo and I think I decided I could do this rodeo thing if I put my mind to it.

I only play golf two to three times a year now, usually up at Cheyenne or if Shane Hanchey or someone wants to play then I'll go play with them. I just burned out on golf and my desire to play isn't there. Even though I don't play a lot I'm still pretty good and that tends to surprise people a bit.

As most people know Shane Hanchey loves his golf, and man, I just kicked his and Hunter Herrin's butts at Cheyenne. I guess I just have to bring them back down to Earth every now and then.

Editor's Note: Hunter Herrin confirmed Clay's win saying, "Yes, it's true. He stuck it on both of us up there!"

Austin Barstow

Tie-down roper Austin Barstow is from Springview, Nebraska, but currently resides in Bozeman, Montana.

Austin got his Associates Degree in Business Managament from Vernon College. He transferred to Montana State University in Bozeman where he's an Assistant Coach for the MSU Rodeo Team.

When he's not coaching, competing, or finishing up his degree Austin passes the time fishing as much as he can.

"Rookie Mistakes"

The first time that I went to compete in an amateur rodeo I was in high school. We headed out for a couple rodeos in one big trip, but this was the first one in the stretch. I was a young kid and I wanted to have fun. Amateur rodeos kind of condone fun so we went out the night before slack and my buddies snuck me into a local bar. I ended up getting pretty liquored up that night. I was just a young guy and we were having fun. We all eventually shuffled back to the trailers and I just crashed.

The next morning slack started at 7am. I'm 17 years old, hung over as hell, and someone starts banging on the trailer door at freaking 7am. I crawled out of bed, threw a saddle on my horse, and just rode into the box.

The calf horse I was riding at the time happened to be pretty cold-backed; if I didn't warm him up real good before running he'd just go to bucking down the arena. Needless to say, I didn't have time to warm him up that morning so we backed in the box cold.

So, here I am; I literally just woke up, wearing the same clothes from last night, no shower, nothing. I am half-tempted to puke off the side of my horse, the sun is shining so brightly I don't even want to keep my eyes open, and I have to compete. Suddenly my decision to have fun the night before didn't seem like the greatest idea I'd ever had.

The calf comes out and I go to swinging my rope. I got about 2-3 strides away from the calf and I could feel my bay horse starting to buck. I just threw my rope, literally just threw it, semi-towards the calf. Somehow I not only managed to rope the calf, but my horse miraculously stopped.

I just kind of bailed out when my horse stopped and somehow it all worked out. My rope was around the calf's head, my horse stopped, and I bailed; it all came tight and I managed to put in a pretty decent run. None of it was supposed to work at all and somehow it all came together.

I was riding back to the box and my dad was like, "Probably should've warmed up that horse a little bit more." I was pretty sure he knew I was totally hung over and that was his way of addressing it. I just mumbled that I probably should have and rode on back to the trailer.

All the other guys knew how hung over I was, there wasn't any hiding it and they all knew how hard we had gone the night before. No one really expected that run to come together like it did, so I guess I got pretty lucky on that one.

D.J. Domangue

D.J. Domangue was a professional bull rider in both the PRCA and the PBR. DJ joined the PRCA in 2003 and qualified for the Wrangler National Finals Rodeo three times.

D.J. first started riding bulls at 13, and the first five years of his career were rough at best, "I think I won like $76 in five years." In his 2nd year at the High School Rodeo Finals, fate stepped in. D.J. broke the wrist on his riding hand and was forced to switch hands - a moment he felt changed his entire career for the better. He never went back to riding with his right hand, "It was either quit or learn to ride left-handed, and quitting wasn't an option."

D.J. competed through his time at Odessa College and upon his graduation turned into a full-time rodeo man. He rode bulls professionally for 12 years and won 11 major rodeos before retiring in March of 2013.

D.J. returned home to Louisiana and is now a diesel mechanic. He's been married for 10 years to his wife Tammy and has a daughter Willow.

"Family"

I think what I miss most about my time in rodeo is just the culture, the family and friends you have on the road. I basically spent 10 years with Colby Yates, Matt Austin, and Bryan Richardson; we traveled all over the country together.

Seeing your buddies every day, every weekend, that was fun. Of course winning was also fun. Winning $20,000-$30,000 in a week is awesome. But then again it also sucks when you're dead broke and trying to scrape change together to go get on another bull. You're beat up, tired, and sore. It's just a constant roller coaster; you're either on a hot streak or you're down in the trenches. It's a physically and mentally demanding sport, no matter how you cut it.

I think I miss the atmosphere more than I miss riding bulls. I can't visualize ever climbing back on a bull. I do a couple schools and camps a year and I go to bull ridings, but I'm like the mom in the stands now. I'm up there twitching my face and cringing when these kids get beat up. It's a rough sport. You've got to have your friends and family there to support you and they have to understand the risks at hand.

I used to travel with Colby Yates and we'd just camp out and write songs with his guitar. Well actually, Colby would write songs and I'd pretend I could play as well as he did. But just sitting around and shooting the shit with your buddies, you can't beat those times. Those are the times I miss the most.

We never really were party-happy guys and didn't see much sense in blowing what little money we had to go get wasted and end up with some stories we'd regret. I was already married so we'd just hang out at the camper and maybe play music for some guys. Sometimes we'd sneak out to some property with a stocked pond, we would crawl through the grass out there so we wouldn't get caught. We'd fish a little, take pictures, throw 'em back, and sneak back out.

We'd hired a driver and man- he would never let us drive. It wasn't a bad idea. We could sleep, rest, whatever and not have to worry about the driving. So we'd just hang out back in the camper and play guitar while he burned up the highways. When you spend that much time with guys they become your family; they just do.

"Jokes On You"

I guess people would say I'm a notorious prankster, I just like making people let loose a bit. People make themselves easy targets too; the more stiff you are, the more I'm going to pick on you.

One time we were in Nashville at an Extreme Bull Riding event. I'd ridden great and was like an 86 or something. I stepped off my bull, landed on my feet, and it was just smooth.

I was walking back to the locker room and realized my groin hurt and it was getting progressively worse. I realized something wasn't right and I needed to check it out. I get back to the locker room, pull my jeans down, and I'm wiggling down my compressions shorts and realized my left nut was about the size of a grapefruit.

Well, everyone leaves their phones in their bags or what not, no sense in riding bulls with a cell phone in your pocket. I wasn't dying, pain-wise, so I decided that every phone I found needed to not only have a picture of my grapefruit-sized testicle, but have it set as their phone background as well. No one was back there so I just started taking pictures and moving from bag to bag, I either made it their screensaver or background.

After my photo shoot I went to the hospital to get an ultrasound done. Nothing was wrong, really. But everybody got back to the locker room and all they could talk about was the gigantic nut that was on their phones.

Another time at the NFR I got Don Gay really good. You know he always wears his vests, right? No matter what, he's got his vest on. We always gave him crap about them. He'd come back to the lounge area, take his vest off, and leave it on the back of a chair or something until he had an interview or had to commentate, and then he'd put it back on.

So I used a whole roll of athletic tape and taped his entire vest to the chair. I just wrapped it around and around until his vest and the chair had become one massive tape wrap. He came back and he was so mad, so freaking mad. He knew it was Cody Whitney, JW Harris, or me, because the three of us were pulling crap like that all the time. I don't think he ever figured out who it was. I guess if he reads this he'll know, but damn it sure was fun!

One year at the National Finals I decided to really shake some shit up. Those stock contractors can be really uptight which makes them perfect prank targets. I grabbed a condom, opened it up, and put a little pickle in it.

They have their own little room at the finals where they hang out and eat. It's pretty easy to get in there and pull some shit. So, I slipped this condom into Harlan Robinson's jacket. He'd just won Bull of the Year and was feeling high and mighty, so he seemed like the perfect choice.

I slid it in his coat pocket and just waited a little bit. I just would come and go; I just waited until he went into that back room. All the contractors were in there so I figured the timing couldn't get much better. I barged in and was like, "Hey man, let me use your phone a second; I've got to text my wife." He wasn't too sure, so I just kept on that my battery had died and I really needed to text her to tell her I was okay, that'd she'd been trying to get ahold of me.

Well, he shoots his hand in his pocket and pulls out this condom with a pickle in it. He face got so red, I thought he was going to explode; it was freaking perfection. That whole room lost it.

Sometimes Cody Whitney and I would go behind those guys and flip the flank straps on the bulls so they were backwards, just little stuff like that to piss them off.

One of the first months I started riding with a helmet I ended up getting knocked out; that's some irony there for you. I think we were in Austin, TX and I was out for about 15 minutes. I remember waking up in the ambulance and hearing my wife's voice. I kept asking the paramedic why she was with me and what was going on. I didn't have the faintest clue I'd even been at a bull riding. So they check me out, conclude that I've sustained yet another concussion, and release me. I remembered what all had happened, the bull I'd gotten on, and all that so they figured I'd be fine to go home with my wife.

We were traveling with some friends so I asked Tammy to give me her cell phone; I decided I was going to call my buddies and mess with them a bit. They finally answered my call and I said, "Yo man, you've got to come pick me up. I'm in this hospital gown and I'm outside the hospital! I ripped all my IVs out and they were trying to send me to surgery. Man, I don't know what's going on; you've got to come get me!"

He kept asking where Tammy was and I just played like I didn't even know who that was. I just told him I'd woken up in the hospital room with a phone and called him for help. I just kept telling him I was outside in the bushes, and as luck would have it, this ambulance came pulling up with all the sirens on which really helped sell things. I started whispering, "Hang on, man; here they come. They're out here looking for me - hurry up!"

They all were at this Eli Young concert that was held after the rodeo; after some whining they said they're coming to get me. What they didn't know was I was actually on the way back to the arena with Tammy, not in a hospital gown in the bushes.

So she and I get back to the arena and I called them back up, "Hey man, you coming to the hospital?" They were almost there and I busted out laughing. I told them they'd better turn around and go back because I was almost at the arena. They were so mad that I'd pulled them out of that concert. I figured if I couldn't be at the concert then they couldn't be there either. We laugh about it now, but they were so mad.

You got to make it fun like that, people get so worn out. When it's the middle of summer, it's hot and everyone is cranky; then towards the finals everybody hurts. You've just got to mix it up and make people laugh; it's the only way to stay sane.

Trevor Haught

Trevor Haught was born in Payson, Arizona and was raised on the Cross F Ranch.

Trevor credits his cousin, bareback rider Klayton Haught, for peaking his interest in rodeo. Clayton came to Trevor's family's ranch just out of high school and was headed to college to ride bareback horses. Trevor says, "I thought that guy was the coolest guy I'd ever met so naturally I started riding bareback horses."

Trevor, while competing in bareback in high school, won 3 state titles. He got a scholarship riding for the rodeo team for New Mexico State. However following a car accident, Trevor switched from riding bareback horses to roping calves.

Trevor currently lives in Dewey, AZ and works on a ranch as a cattleman and trains roping horses. He continues competing at amateur rodeos as well as being a pick-up man.

"Lion Tamer"

My family kind of settled the Payson, Arizona area and I'm pretty proud of that. I think my great-great-great-grandfather was the second person to move there and sort of establish things. My family ran a ranch in Little Green Valley and at the time they called it the Haught Ranch; I think the Earnharts own it now. My grandfather and my dad were born there, so it's a pretty neat little place for me.

My great-grandfather's name was Sam Haught and he was kind of the head honcho there. One day, sometime in the 1930's, they had this drunk cowboy come riding into the ranch from town proclaiming he'd seen a plane crash and a huge African lion.

Well, no one believed him because he was drunk. After two or three days of listening to his persistent story, they all agreed to ride up there and check things out. This big group of guys headed out to go investigate this supposed plane crash site and see what the now-sober man was talking about.

I can't remember if both the pilots died or if one walked away, but they rode up there and sure enough there was a lion there. They didn't know it at the time but it was "Leo the Lion" from MGM Grand. He was the lion that roared for the MGM credits in movies, basically MGM's mascot.

My great-grandfather decided they couldn't leave the lion there to die, so they skidded this cage with a lion in it all the way back to the ranch. They got back to the house and the guys start feeding this lion. They had no idea if it was tamed or trained, so to speak; they were all scared to death of him. This huge African lion in the middle of Arizona.

Well, the lion started getting drawn down and really sick. Pappy Haught, my great-grandfather, was going to treat the lion but no one wanted to get ahold of it. So they came up with the grand idea of turning this lion loose and roping him, one guy climbed up on the cage and released the latch and out comes this African lion.

They managed to rope him and had him stretched every which way. Pappy Haught had to put a knee on his neck while he went to doctoring on him. I mean they had no idea this lion was tamed but they weren't going to let it lie there and die.

So they nursed the lion back to health. I think he had ringworm or something like that. A few weeks later they got a letter from MGM asking if the company could come pick-up their lion. These trainers came out from Hollywood and picked him up.

Apparently that lion survived a couple plane crashes, a train crash, and a car accident; just a bunch of really crazy stuff. But I don't think anything can hold up to my great-granddad roping him.

People always ask the question, "If you could go back in time, where would you go?" I say I'd go right there so I could see them rope a lion in the middle of Arizona.

Editor's Note: "Jackie" was the second MGM lion, commonly referred to as "Leo the Lion". "Jackie" served as the MGM lion from 1928-1956, surviving two train wrecks, an earthquake, an explosion on set, and a plane crash.

"Drunk On A Plane"

When I was 17, just before I went to the high school finals, I went to the 4th of July rodeo in Taylor, AZ. They get like 10,000 fans there so it's a big deal around here. It was a big deal to me then and still is now.

Well, I won the rodeo that year. I got some recognition from the local guys because I'd kind of established I was worth something. So, they all started giving me the time of day and offered to take me out on the road with them.

I started traveling around with this group of guys who called themselves "The Arizona Wild Bunch". I don't know why roughstock riders have to name themselves, but we do. We went to a handful of rodeos in Texas and New Mexico, and we were on a bit of a stretch. One night we were in Lubbock, TX and this guy JT and I were just doing really well. He won the rodeo and I'd placed, so we were feeling good.

We decided to head out and celebrate. Somehow they had hooked 17-year-old me up with a fake ID, which was just like gold. It's pretty amazing what a fake ID can do for a 17-year-old. We all headed off to the bar and we just were having a great time. I was like, "Man, I love this stuff right here!"

The next night we were in New Mexico and I placed again, so I have a pocketful of money, a fake ID, and I am having the time of my life. We stayed out all night. I'm traveling with guys who are in their late 20's to early 40's, and they're showing me how to party.

We were staying at this guy's place because he'd had some bareback horses he'd let us climb on. Well, I woke up and I thought it was really early because it was dark in the house. I walked downstairs and there was this guy in the living room. I realized he hadn't been there the night before; I had no idea who he was and he's jus sitting in the living room.

He asked me how it was going and I was like, "Umm…pretty good. I think we had a hell of a time last night." He asked if we were up in Albuquerque today and I said, "Yes sir, we are. " And he looked at me real slowly and asked, "Well, what time is that perf today?" I looked at him sort of puzzled, "I think it's at like 1 or 1:30." So he just keeps asking me questions: "How did you get here?" "That silver Dodge outside, sir."

He turns to me and goes, "Well it's 1 o'clock now, that performance is about two hours away, and there's no silver Dodge outside. " Well, I about shit myself and I started running around the house looking for the guys. Turns out those guys had left JT and I there, I don't know if they left us because we'd been winning and they weren't or what, but those other two guys left us there!

We ended having to buy a plane ticket home from Albuquerque and we about drank that plane out of beer. I ended up sitting next to a guy who was a professional chef; he'd been on TV, makes 6-figures, that kind of chef. Well, he liked to drink beer and have fun, so we got really drunk together and started talking.

I fully credit that guy for changing my whole outlook on riding bucking horses. He talked about food and cooking with such a passion, that it just got me to thinking. I realized being a cowboy wasn't just about drinking beer, chewing Copenhagen, sleeping around, or partying; it was about passion.

I quit traveling with those guys. We're still friendly, but that conversation and that series of events kind of changed everything for me. I kind of wish I hadn't been drunk because I probably could have learned a little bit more, but if we hadn't been drunk we probably wouldn't have had the conversation that we did.

I wish I could remember that guy's name, but I can't. If I could I'd call him up and thank him for changing my whole life right there. Seventeen, drunk on a plane, and with a fake ID. I owe that guy the biggest thank you; he just made me look at things and the life I was living in a whole new way.

What scared me was just leading a normal life; the last thing I want is a job. I want to do what I love to do, and do it 100% because I love it. I get along with horses and cattle way better than I get along with people. I guess that's what that chef taught me. I think the last thing I ever expected was a professional chef teaching me about being a cowboy, and showing me the kind of life I wanted to lead.

Colby Yates

Colby Yates was a professional bull rider for both the PRCA and Professional Bull Riders. In his six years on the PBR Built Ford Tough Series, Colby won three events; his earnings topped out at over half a million dollars. He qualified for six PBR Finals and one NFR.

In 2011 Colby went on to win the Iron Cowboy at Cowboys Stadium; that same year he also released his CD "Right Amount of Renegade".

After obtaining a staggering 38 concussions in his 14-year career, Colby decided to hang up his bull rope in August 2012.

Today, Colby works in the oil and gas industry of Texas. He and his wife Katie and their son Cutter make their home just outside of Fort Worth, TX.

"Iron Cowboy"

The Iron Cowboy event was going to take place at Cowboys Stadium in my hometown of Dallas, TX. I was just outside of making the cut by one guy; I was right there on the bubble. Robson Palermo had gotten injured the weekend before in Oklahoma City and had messed up his ribs. He was going to the doctor on the Wednesday before the event, so my chance of riding depending on the outcome of his appointment.

Jay Daughtery had called me up and said, "Robson's not sure about Dallas. He's going to the doctor and we'll know from there." I was like, "Jay, tell him he can't go!" No offense to Robson, I was bummed he was hurt, but I wanted to ride in my hometown event. I was just pumped about the possibility of even getting to go, but man, I wanted it. The idea of riding bulls in Cowboys Stadium in front of a hometown crowd, you just can't beat that.

So that Wednesday afternoon Jay calls me up and says, "Hey, you're in; he's not going." I just went, "Hallelujah!" Again, Robson's a really good friend so I wasn't happy he was hurt; I was just so glad for the opportunity.

It was only the second year they'd done the Iron Cowboy deal and the format is a bracket-system. Instead of facing lots of guys and the top 15 coming back for a short-go, you just keep going head-to-head with one other rider. You didn't even have to make the buzzer; it was just whoever was closest to eight seconds. If you made the buzzer, then it was who scored the highest. It was just something new and different with the opportunity for some really big money and I wanted it.

At the time we were living in Sulphur Springs, TX, our ranch was on the market but we were still based out of there. After Jay called me, Katie and I sent Cutter to stay with my aunt and uncle, and off we went to Dallas. I was probably speeding like a maniac the whole time. I didn't have to be there by a certain time that day, but I wanted to get there as fast as possible.

We got there and I was just like a kid on Christmas. I didn't want to get 50 feet from the building the whole time I was there. I was doing all the daily activities for the PBR and running all over that stadium. I swear, it's like a mile around that thing and it didn't even faze me; I was absolutely jumping out of my skin. I was so pumped up about being there in the middle of things and I'd drawn really well. To be honest, I don't think I ever really calmed down the whole weekend.

We were doing the rehearsal for the introductions and it was surreal to be standing in the middle of Cowboys Stadium. I just had this really good feeling about things; it's this feeling I'd only ever had about five times in my career. I had a really good gut feeling I was going to win. It felt like I knew the win was absolutely going to happen. In the past that feeling had lead to wins, so my adrenaline levels were off the charts. I was jumpy; it felt like I'd had about 10 Red Bulls and 24 hours of sleep.

Even back in the locker room, before things got started, the energy was just on a whole other level. All the guys were psyched on the format and it made the competitive edge more extreme. It was a totally different atmosphere than any other event; everyone was dead-focused on what they had to do and who they were up against. It's pretty inspiring as a bull rider to see and feel that kind of energy in a space. Just to experience and be in that moment when everyone's on the same page, those times are really significant.

That night about 40,000 people packed that stadium to watch us ride. It reminded me of the first time I'd ever gone to the NFR. It was absolutely crazy. That stadium means a lot to me since I'm from there. I love watching the Cowboys and I love being from Texas. It was just the real deal and I was in the middle of it. At that point in my career I didn't really get that swept up in stuff, but it was just crazy. Just the energy of being in the building with all those fans was unreal.

During the introductions they went over the top with the pyro and the lights, and when they announced my name and where I was from those fans went nuts. You could literally feel the room vibrating and every time they mentioned I was from Ft. Worth the crowd would just roar. The hair was standing up on the back of my neck and my adrenaline was spiking again. It was almost surreal. It was just an awesome feeling.

I got a fresh bull for my first match-up; the bull I was supposed to ride had been injured. I had zero experience with this second bull, but I was so pumped up I didn't even care. My first out I was up against Travis Briscoe; I had this bull and I just knew I was going to dominate. This bull went to the right, away from my hand, and usually that was bad news on my end. I didn't care, I knew I had him. That ride felt easy; I was so on. I just thought, "This is my night. It's gonna happen." I felt invincible.

I was 88 points on him and the second I hit the dirt the crowd just went nuts, and that momentum kept building for every ride and every bracket. My adrenaline was just off the charts. I could feel the sweat dripping down my back; my shirt was probably soaked and I didn't even realize it. At one point the announcer said something like, "It's a lovely evening out in here Cowboy Stadium with a cool night of only 70 degrees!" I remember thinking, "Bullshit!" It felt like a 100 degrees down there on that dirt.

In the quarterfinals I went up against JB Mauney; he had drawn Chicken on a Chain and I'd drawn Carillo Cartel, just two powerhouse bulls. Chicken on a Chain is this big bull with lots of presence and Carillo Cartel is fast and flashy. Well JB goes out and rides for 90 points and then it's my turn.

Climbing down into the chute I knew Carillo Cartel would buck into my hand, so I felt confident. This was an epic match-up with JB and I; I knew for a fact that I'd better take a boot to mine to make things happen. I was in the chute thinking, "Alright, do or die. You'd better come at it with all you've got." I HAD to ride this bull and it HAD to be for more than 90 points. 90-point rides aren't too common, but I just trusted my gut and nodded my head.

It seemed like slow motion, I remember spurring him so aggressively that it felt like my knee kept coming up by my ear. I threw caution to the wind; I could not and would not come off of this bull. When I heard the faint sound of the buzzer, everything snapped back into full force. I hit the dirt and I knew it was a career-changing ride; one I'd never forget. I ended up being 92.25 on him, beating JB, and moving onto the semifinals.

So, it comes down to the semifinals and I'm up against Valdiron de Oliveira. I was up first and I bucked off in 3.2 seconds. Most cowboys would have thought it was all over at that point, but somehow I knew I'd be okay. I'm not really sure that made sense at the time, but that's what I was feeling.

Valdiron bucked off in 3.3 and I still knew I'd beat him. They have these buzzers you can hit to protest timing, if you think you actually lasted 8 seconds or your opponent didn't. Valdiron is my friend, but it is a competition and I swore I outrode him. I whipped my head up and around, frantically searched for the closest buzzer. I finally got to one and hit that thing so hard I'm surprised I didn't break my hand.

The judges have to review every protest call so they're looking at the footage and timing his ride over and over, playing it in slow motion and frame by frame. Most people would have been jumping out of their skin with anticipation, but I knew I'd beaten him. I just needed the judges to see that and rule in my favor. They ended up making the call that he bucked off in 3.0 and I ended advancing to the finals against Austin Mier.

Austin was on the infamous Bushwacker, who was just a nasty bull, and I drew I'm A Gangster. Austin was the top seed in the tournament, but I knew I just had to hang on longer than he did. If he was 5 seconds, all I had to be was 5.1. I was up first and lasted just 2.45 seconds on I'm A Gangster; he is this big, powerful bull and just got me off.

I was standing there waiting for Austin to go and hoping that gut feeling I'd had was right; I needed this to be my night. Sweat was still pouring off of me and things still seemed to be moving in slow motion. So, Austin climbs down in the chute and nods his head, Bushwacker freaking launched out of the chute, and Austin popped off at 2.34 seconds.

Just like that, I had the Iron Cowboy title and $50,000 in my pocket. I knew as soon as I saw Austin hit the dirt and looked at the clock, it had all come together. It was unreal. That stadium got so loud when they announced that the hometown guy had won it all. I just knew it was going to be my night and it had been; no doubts.

I threw my rope down and took off to the podium for a quick interview about winning, and then they presented me with the Iron Cowboy buckle. I straight hustled out there while trying to catch my breath and gain my composure. They put that buckle in my hands and it was just amazing. I was almost in a trance looking down at it, "2011 Iron Cowboy Champion" and it was all mine.

Afterwards I felt a little bad I didn't actually ride two of the six bulls I got on for the full 8 seconds, but with the format I didn't need to. Cody Lambert told me, "Winning is winning. You won first and that's it." It came to down to a little bit of luck and a whole lot of effort to make things happen, as well as trusting that gut feeling.

It was easily one of the most surreal moments of my career. I can't explain the feeling I had going into things, but I just had no doubt that I was going to win. It was just crazy in that stadium; the fans were loud, the bulls were rank, and the competition was exceptional. Those things combined to create this energy and it just drove me so much. I don't think my adrenaline has ever been that super charged.

Any athlete who experiences a moment like that knows their career is complete. Doesn't matter what else you go on to accomplish, that moment lasts forever.

"Gonna Be A Wild Ride"

Not many people know this but I'm terrified of horses; the irony of a cowboy being terrified of horses is not lost on me. When I was a kid I'd be put on these ponies that weren't very broke and they'd take off with me and it scared me. Call it imprinting or what not but I've been scared of horses ever since.

People always say, "So, let me get this straight, you're scared of horses but you're not scared of bulls?" I think my deal with horses is that they're smart. Horses know what they're doing. When it comes to bulls everything is just going so fast they don't really have time to think that fast, they are a bit slower mentally. I feel more in control on top of a bull and when they're done bucking all they want to do is go back to the pen and eat. I just never seem to have control in horse situations.

At most rodeos you're required to take a victory lap...on a horse. I'm not super forthcoming about the fact I'm scared of horses so I always just tried to either suck it up and deal with it or pray that I won 2nd so I didn't have to ride a freaking horse.

One time I got on this barrel horse and his owner was like, "Oh, just take him in the arena there and lope him around a few times." Well, I didn't know how psycho barrel horses got so I didn't think it was a big deal. I got behind the ally of the arena and this horse lost his mind. He reared up, I flew off the back of him and he kicked the hell out of me. I swore right there and then I'd never get on another barrel horse for the rest of my life.

Like I said, every time you win a round at a rodeo, well most rodeos, you have to ride out and do a victory lap; I've had some really bad victory laps. I definitely have opted to go out and run a lap versus riding one. One year at the National Western in Denver I was 86 points on this bull, but I thought that I was 85 or something. Another guy, Casey, had ridden and was 86 points so I thought, "Phew, I don't have to ride the damn horse." I hadn't won as much money but I was so glad I didn't have to ride.

Next thing I know they're wrapping up the bull riding and with the victory lap you've got to get in the ally to go into the arena pretty quick; those victory laps have to be almost an immediate thing. They start yelling, "Yates! Yates! Get on this horse!" I literally felt the blood drain from my face and I'm screaming back, "No, no! Casey won! He was 86!" Come to find out we'd tied for the win, just my luck.

And do you think they'd have two horses? Nope. At Denver they have these white horses and since they only expect one guy to win that's all that was standing there. We ended up having to ride double and we're both still wearing our bull riding spurs, chaps, and vests. I told Casey there was no way I was climbing on the back of this horse. I was going to be in the saddle and that was that. I figured that I'd have more control versus praying for dear life holding on behind Casey. He didn't give a crap so we both climbed aboard and took off out of the ally.

As soon as we take off the girl who owns the horse hollers, "Watch out for him! He bucks!" I realized what she'd said and I don't think I've ever put that many swear words into a single sentence. So naturally I clamp down even more and what would you know, this thing starts bucking.

A bunch of guys had lined up on the back of the chutes to watch this victory lap; they all knew I was terrified to ride horses so it was always a good show. Some Australian photographer took pictures of it and the reins are up by my ears and my butt is off the saddle about six inches. I was just gripping, white knuckling that saddle horn for all I was worth.

My mouth is even open in the picture, probably cursing that horse, his owner, and every second that lead up to that moment.

Casey is back behind me and he is laughing his ass off, he thought it was hysterical. As soon as we got towards the end of the arena, Casey just started spurring this horse and trying to entice her, so of course she came unglued. They could've been 90 in the bronc riding on her. She was kicking up over her head and I'm just hanging on for dear life.

At one point in this victory lap turned bull ride, I am actually over the saddle horn on this horse's neck and Casey is now in the saddle. I didn't let go of the saddle horn though so I'm on this horse's neck basically riding my arm. This horse is just full steam ahead and I swore I was going to be on the injured list before it was all said and done.

Somehow I ended up back on top of Casey, basically sitting in his lap, and he wiggles back behind the saddle. This horse is starting to lose steam and the announcer is just feeding the crowd, calling out what he thinks our score is going to be when this ride from hell comes to an end. Once we got back into the saddle where we were supposed to be, I just bailed out, dropped the reins and bailed out. Poor Casey was just left hanging there, back behind the saddle, with nothing to hold on to!

Another time, I'd been invited down to Chris Shivers' place to go hog hunting. They know I'm terrified of horses and promised they'd give me this old broke horse, basically a kid's horse, Ol' Blue. I should've known it wasn't going to be that simple, but I decided I'd give it a go so they'd quit giving me grief.

After some really questionable looks from Ross Coleman's dad, he found out I was scared of horses, and we headed out. It wasn't long before we came to a creek. It was a pretty steep drop down to the water and I've only been on this horse one time. I've been riding all of about 5 minutes on a 4,000-acre ranch and this is what comes up, of course. So we ride up on this gully and I'm going, "Whoooooa, Yates don't do water, Yates does not do water." It wasn't just a creek; it was a bit more monumental than that.

All my buddies just take off across the "creek" and I'm about 100 yards behind them and finally I decided I'd better just get on or they were going to leave me. So, Ol' Blue and I ease our way across and then he decided he wanted to catch up with his buddies, and I sure as hell didn't want him to! Well, here goes sturdy Ol' Blue. He takes off, catches up to everyone and keeps right on going. Yet again, I've got the reins back by my ears and finally he runs out of air and slows down. I could hear the guys just laughing behind me.

Finally, we come across this big herd of hogs. There were probably about 20 of them and we had five or six dogs with us. The dogs went nuts and they just bolted and those hogs scattered. Mike White takes after one, Chris Shivers takes after one, I take after one, and a couple other guys did the same. I realized I didn't have a clue what I was going to do with mine if I ever caught it. We ended up back in the woods and luckily Mike came and rescued me. We got this hog tied up and I reached down to grab his back legs. As soon as I do, the dogs let go of this hog and he came straight after me. "Freaking great, just my luck." They ended up catching him again just as I skirted around the tree.

So, we get that hog taken care of and Mike takes off after another one. He's hollering back at me to hurry up and help him. I'm watching him and all of sudden Mike just vanishes. I get up there and realize there is probably a 50 foot drop down to this river. I mean it is straight down, "The Man From Snowy River" style. I see Mike slide down the side of the riverbank; his horse was basically sitting and sliding and then he started swimming across this river. I'm sitting there thinking, "Yates sure as hell don't do that!"

I'm screaming at Mike that I'm not going down there and he's screaming at me to hurry up and get down there, because the dogs are all in the river going after this hog and he couldn't get the dogs off the hog by himself. Mike ends up swimming his horse back into the river and starts grabbing the dogs out of the water and plopping them across his lap. I realized I probably needed to get down there and help him out so I eased "Ol' Blue" to the edge of this bank, squeezed, and started screaming; I swear I screamed the whole way down.

It was definitely not my proudest moment.

Mike finally gets the hog roped and he's hanging onto to this angry hog and the dogs. He wraps the rope around the hog's tusks and hands it to me and tells me to go back up the embankment with the hog. I looked at Mike like he was kidding. I swore he was joking; we take all the hogs we catch back and process them though so I knew he wasn't.

I grabbed the rope, wrapped it around my horn, and "Ol' Blue" and I went hooping and hollering back up this embankment. I took him up there and was like, "Mike, what the hell are we supposed to do now?" We get back to the trailer and Chris and I get all these hogs contained in the trailer and Mike shuts the freaking door on us. Chris says, "Get in there, cut the straps, and get behind the gate as fast as you can."

That part actually didn't end up being that bad, I was more comfortable doing that then riding! It actually was probably one of my better experiences with horses; in the grand scheme of things Ol' Blue took pretty good care of me. I actually went back and went out with those guys a couple more times so long as they promised I could ride Ol' Blue. He and I were on the same level at some points and he clearly knew I didn't have a clue what I was doing.

The day Mike sold that horse I swore I'd never go back and I haven't. I can't believe he went and sold my horse on me!

"A Day Late and A Dollar Short"

I guess it was sometime in September and we were up in Washington, it was toward the end of the season. I had a broken ankle, a broken arm with a cast on it, and my jaw was wired shut too. I was really busted up. I was in the Top 15 at the time and figured nothing could really go wrong, I just wanted a little bit better seat going into the NFR. Just when you think nothing else is going to go wrong it does.

I had this bull of Mike Corey's and he was a wild little 4-year old. Right out of the chutes he jumped up in the air and when he came down, he landed straight on top of me. He smothered me to the point it didn't even look like I was on his back.

He ended up breaking my collarbone in three places, just shattered it. I was going to get on my re-ride bull since I automatically got one because the bull fell down. My shoulder was just on fire at this point, I knew something was probably wrong but didn't really want to think about it. I told Matt Austin to go rope my re-ride bull up for me, I'd be over there in a minute. He kind of looked at me funny, I wasn't the guy who expected other people to do my work for me.

My shirt was torn open and my collarbone was stretching out against my skin, with this big ol' knot that was not where it was supposed to me. Matt was like, "Dude, you broke you collarbone." I remember thinking; "Son of a bitch…" and I just went home. I didn't want to go home, I had all those nagging injuries though so it probably was the best option.

I drove over 30 hours home that night. I had like five Red Bulls while driving; I was shaking like a dog when I got home. I didn't know any different but I knew it was working. Looking back I'm lucky I didn't go into cardiac arrest or anything. I mean my jaw was wired shut still so I didn't even have solid food in my stomach; just mainstreaming Red Bull on a basically empty stomach.

I got home and I had like two months to heal up, you get a little bit of a break between the end of the season and when Finals start. They ballpark it as 6-8 weeks for your collarbone to heal up so I had like three weeks to heal up and try to work my way back up.

I knew I was in a time crunch and I needed to do some supernatural healing. I ended up buying this $3,000 machine cause I wanted to go to the Finals. I knew I was going to have to go to the final couple of rodeos to really make it happen. This machine was like a bone stimulator and you're supposed to wear it 2-3 times a day. I figure more is better, so I'm sticking it on like 5-6 times a day. I was drinking this Mother Nature shit that's like five different drinks that all make you want to puke. I was drinking those things like 10 times a day. It was just terrible; I was trying so hard to get back. If there was anything I thought would speed up the healing process I did it.

I ended up coming back at the last event before Finals and it was about 3-4 weeks after I'd broken my collarbone. I had to win at this point; I had been set so far back from where I had been. I was in like the 21st or 22nd place, and I needed to be in the Top 15. I kind of did the math and knew I had to win like $5,000 or something to get in there and make the NFR.

I ended up winning like $7,500, but still didn't make the finals. In the PRCA the ground money doesn't count towards finals so I was out of it because of that; I couldn't have missed making it by more than two spots. I won 2nd at the event and still missed it!

So here I am thinking about all the money I spent on that machine and how much of that Mother Nature crap I drank and I still didn't get it done. But that's rodeo life you know, a day late and a dollar short.

Richmond Champion

Richmond Champion lives in Stephenville, Texas and attended Tarleton State University.

Richmond climbed on his first bareback horse in 2010, the summer before his senior year of high school, and has been a PRCA cardholder ever since.

When he's not on the road he's helping his TSU Rodeo Team coach with team practice and helps mentor the students on the team. Richmond likes to rope, hunt, fish, and ride horses in his spare time (which he doesn't have much of).

Richmond won The American in March 2014, instantly winning a million dollar check. He qualified for the 2014 National Finals Rodeo, won Rounds 5 and 7, and placed in three additional rounds.

"It's been a crazy, awesome experience ever since I put my hand in a bareback rigging."

"Hallowed Ground"

In early 2012 my Uncle Perry was diagnosed with pancreatic cancer and he passed away in December of that same year. He was always one of my biggest rodeo supporters, hands down. When I was on the road he would always call to check in and see how things were going. He had a radio station in New Mexico and he'd always have me call into the station and practice my interviews. He'd record them and send them to me so I could see where I could improve. He was always just a big part of really helping me to be not just another rodeo cowboy. He helped me learn how to handle the media aspect of things too.

When my dad and my uncle were younger they always competed at Ellensburg so it was a special place for them. They both went to Washington State so the western part of Washington has always had an influence on my family.

In 2013 I was headed to Ellensburg to compete, my grandparents live there so my whole family came along. At that point in my rodeo career, I hadn't won a major rodeo yet. I was sitting around 30th in the world going to Ellensburg and I needed a big short-go somewhere to make things happen.

We headed up a couple days early to spread my uncle's ashes at my grandparents place. When we were done my dad handed me a little corner of the bag with some of my uncle's ashes and said, "Might as well put some of these in the arena tomorrow." I thought it would be really cool to do since the Ellensburg rodeo meant so much to my uncle so I told my dad I'd be honored to do it.

The next day was the long-go at Ellensburg and my brother and I got there a little bit early; it was pretty quiet and we had some privacy. He and I walked down to the bucking chutes and let the ashes trickle out onto the ground right in front of the chutes.

My first horse that day was from Calgary Stampede, a nice little mare that everyone tends to have solid luck on and I was excited to have her. My whole family was in the stands along with my dad's college buddies, and obviously my uncle was there too. This little mare reared up and out of the chutes and bailed out. She leapt out of that chute with such force she never even touched the ground where we spread my uncle's ashes.

I was 88 on her and it was enough to win the long round. When I was walking back to the chutes I locked eyes with my brother as if to say, "This is too weird." You can call it coincidence or whatever but I think it was more than that.

In the short-round I drew a horse called "Big Easy", but there's nothing easy about riding "Big Easy". He's strong and in my opinion, one of the strongest horses going. I wasn't necessarily excited to have him. My brother and dad kept saying, "What do you have to worry about? You're in Uncle Perry's house now."

I'd always done well at header rodeos but could never clinch it in the short-round so I was pretty nervous to have the top bucking horse going in. I nodded for Big Easy and out we went. At about the five second mark my chaps broke, just snapped. So here I am I'm trying to spur with my chaps around my ankles, that makes a couple extra pounds on each foot.

When I finished I was 85, third in the short-go, and won the average. It had all finally started to click. After everything had calmed down I started thinking about it and I chuckled to myself thinking about how it would be just like my Uncle Perry to make it so my chaps broke.

The whole experience still gives me goosebumps. It was just awesome to have my whole family there and to feel my uncle's presence. It was a really special experience for me to have my first big win there. With everything else going on, the win brought it all full circle. Seems like ever since then it's all gone to the next level. My career has just been on such a good roll.

Ellensburg went terrible for me this year (2014) but the feeling I got when I walked into that arena was pretty incredible. It almost had a calming effect on me; just knowing my uncle was there. It's a feeling I can't really translate into words.

Troy Crowser

Troy Crowser hails from Whitewood, South Dakota. He began riding saddle broncs professionally in 2010 and won Rookie of the Year that same year.

Troy also qualified for the College National Finals three times, qualified for the Canadian Finals, and won the Badlands Circuit Finals as well.

When Troy isn't on the road he's helping his dad, Scott Crowser, on their family ranch as well as breaking colts and roping.

"Never Gonna Make It"

The 4th of July run of my rookie year was really intense. It was the first time Cole Elshere, Tyrel Larson, Chancey Miller, and I were just going really hard. I don't know how but we got split up in our travels. Cole decided that we should enter rodeos in Red Lodge, Montana and Livingston, Montana in the same day. I didn't want to do it; I just didn't think we could make it from one to the other in the same day.

Anyway, we entered both of them. Cole said he had talked to some older guys who had done it no problem. Apparently things were different now. I showed up to the first rodeo with our big van and I was talking with the guys. The only other guys who'd decided to try and make the same run were the Wright brothers. They had a little plane flying them back and forth from Livingston to Red Lodge. I tried to get on the plane but there wasn't room or something.

I had a not-so-great horse drawn there too. I didn't even want to get on him to be honest, Earl the Squirrel was his name. I'd ridden him at the College Finals that year and he had kind of run off then turned back, and as soon as the clock hit 8 seconds he decided to turn back and be the rankest thing you ever saw.

Well, I decided I should go try him because everyone was telling me he had been having better outs. I got there and Jake Costello told me I needed to get the heck out of there. I had a really solid horse drawn in Livingston, but I was already there so I figured I'd just ride him anyways. It ended up not even being worth it. Jake ended up being right...

In the meantime, Cody Wright was trying to get me on their little plane to Livingston, but the pilot kept saying no. I don't know if it was weight or a matter of paperwork, but it just wasn't happening. So luckily Red Lodge let me buck first and then I jumped in that van and took off for Livingston.

I drove as fast as I possibly could. I had Aaron Ferguson on the phone; he was a bullfighter there and was keeping me updated. When I had service I'd call him for an update on how things were moving along, Now that van tops out at 97 mph so I couldn't go any faster than that. I got about 15-20 minutes out and Aaron called me and said, "You're not going to make it." I was pleading with him to do anything he could to delay, since I was almost there.

I'm not sure he actually did anything, but he said he would try. I ended up pulling in there and they'd delayed things by letting the clown act do something to kill some time. I flew into the rodeo grounds and that road in there was rough. I don't know why it was so rough, but I'm bouncing this van all over the road. I was going way too fast and probably killing the suspension in the process.

This lady at the front gate jumps out to tell me to slow down or something. I'm hanging out the window yelling at her to move so I didn't run her over. I felt so bad about it but I had to do it. I just kept going. I pulled in right behind the chutes and grabbed my saddle; I already had my chaps on and everything. I ran up there and they were bucking the second bronc with two more until me!

I saddled him up, trying to catch my breath in the process, and bucked without stretching or anything. I think I ended up splitting 3rd and 4th there, but it was quite the adventure to get there that's for sure. I called Cole and was like, "Never again man, never again."

Another time we were up in Nampa, Idaho. Cole and I had driven from Morris, Manitoba to Nampa. We rode there and I'd made the short round. We left Nampa and drove straight through to Salinas the next morning. At that time the Cervi Rodeo Company had a plane from Salinas back to Nampa that night for the short round and I really needed to be on it. It was the only way to make it back in time. So we were up in Salinas that day and I needed to be back in Nampa that night. I don't know how I really expected that to work out smoothly.

So I caught up to the Cervis and made sure I had a spot on the plane. They assured me that I did and we were good. The next morning we were sitting in our hotel room, which was just outside of Salinas. We stopped by to pick up a buddy who'd flown in, then were all just taking a nap and killing some time. Well the Cervis called me up and said my spot on the plane back to Nampa had been taken. He was sorry but apparently a barrel racer and a steer wrestler had already had our spots on the plane, they just hadn't known about it.

In a shear panic I start calling every kind of jet company or private plane company I could find. I had no idea what I was doing and they're quoting me ridiculous prices like $10,000 and $20,000. Finally someone transferred me to a guy who had a plane and he transferred me to another guy who did little flights back and forth like we needed. He was going to charge us $4,200 to fly back but it was going to take like three hours. I didn't really know if that was going to work or not but we really didn't have any other choice. I talked to Bryce Miller and we realized that even if we didn't make the rodeo we still had to pay him. It was just a chance we had to take.

We get to the Salinas rodeo and it's supposed to start at 1pm. I don't know what happened there, but they didn't get started until 2pm. We found the stock contractors and luckily they agreed to let us buck first, since we had to get back to that plane. Bryce rode and got bucked off. I rode and my horse ended up turning around backwards and I got a re-ride. I gave up the re-ride and found out later my buddy made it back to the short-round on that horse.

Seth Hardwick drove us to the airport right after we rode and we get on the plane no problem. It's like a three hour flight so we just kicked back. The rodeo in Nampa starts at 7:30 and I'd looked at my phone and thought we were fine, "Shoot man, it's only 7!" I didn't really know what time zone we were in though, or that the time zone was going to switch between Salinas and Nampa.

So we got closer to Nampa and I looked at my phone and realized it was an hour ahead and I'm just like, "Oh crap…" We were supposed to have a guy coming to the airport to pick up us, so as we're getting ready to land I texted him and told him that we were there. He texted me back and said, "So you guys have bags you have to get out of baggage claim or what?" I realized rather quickly that he was at the Boise Airport and we were at the private Nampa airport.

We've already landed at that point and we just figured we were screwed; we landed right at 8:15. I'd called my buddy Kaleb Asay because I knew he was hanging out at the rodeo. He jumped in Wesley Silcox's pickup and camper and drove very, very fast to the airport. It was only like six blocks from the rodeo with like a 30mph speed limit.

We'd even run in the airport and asked the one guy in this entire private airport if there was a car we could borrow, he'd just looked at us all confused and said, "Uhh, not really." So we took off walking up the road in hopes of meeting Kaleb halfway at least and we could hear him coming. Bryce is just over there going, "We didn't make it, we're screwed, we're done." I'm next to him thinking, "Come on, man, let's try to be a little bit more positive." I was sure he was right but I sure was hoping for the best.

I kept calling the guys at the rodeo and I couldn't quite hear them with the crowd and all but I made out that they had the clown act going. He kept asking if we were almost there and I just kept telling him we were. So we met Kaleb, hopped in the truck, and we pulled in there right as they bucked the first horse. Our horses were already loaded and we were running, halfway throwing on our gear as we went.

We didn't even known what we'd drawn going into things. I ended up being 2nd in the short go and 3rd in the rodeo. Bryce was like 4th in the short and 5th in the average. We actually made enough to pay for our flight and still pocket some money so I guess it worked out all right. We just cut it a little too close for my comfort. I'd never want to do it again, but it worked. You didn't even have time to be nervous, just a huge sigh of relief when my saddle got put on that horse.

For some reason it just always seems like we're running late...

Bryan Richardson

Bryan Richardson was born and raised in Dallas, TX. Bryan started riding when he was 13 years old, frequently attending local youth rodeos. Bryan continued his rodeo ways all through high school and college, Bryan turned down multiple college rodeo scholarships so that he would have more freedom when it came to his career.

Bryan bought both his PBR and PRCA cards as soon he turned 18. Though he spent much of his rookie year injured, he managed to finish out the year in the #2 rookie spot.
When Bryan was just 20 years old, his 3rd year competing professionally, he qualified for his very first National Finals Rodeo.

Bryan holds several records to his name including the Bullnanza Champion and the Lazy E Arena high-score record with a 95-point ride. He was the only 2-time Texas Stampede Champion at Dallas American Airlines Arena, where he also holds the arena record with a 95-point ride.
Bryan also tied the 20-year-old arena record of 92 points in Salinas, California; a title he shares with Bobby Delvecchoi who set it in 1978.

With notable wins to his name such as Texas Circuit and Texas Circuit Finals Champion, Cow Palace, Pendleton Round-Up, Ellensburg, Red Bluff, Pecos, Abilene (3x Champion), Austin, and Cody, WY (2x Champion), Bryan would go on to qualify for the Wrangler National Finals three times.

Bryan also had a solid career with the PBR, winning Salinas, San Francisco, Sikeston, MO, and the ABBI Finals; Bryan would head to the Professional Bull Riders Finals twice. He retired from rodeo in 2012.

Today Bryan makes his home outside Dallas, TX with his wife and two sons. In addition to working for North Texas Pipe, Bryan is also a hunting guide in South Texas on Texas Hidden Springs Ranch, owned by Keith Warren.

"Long Shot"

The time I qualified for my 1st NFR was just an unreal experience; it took a lot to get there though.

I was traveling all over, you know just traveling with different guys really. I was sitting 6th or 7th in the world by springtime and ended up pulling my groin muscle and was forced to sit out.

By the time winter rolled around I'd joined up with Colby Yates and Philip Elkins, and at this point, having steady travel partners tended to make things easier. The tour finale was at the MGM Grand. I was just a kid and didn't really know if I'd ever make it to the National Finals, but I knew I'd made it this far and I didn't want to miss out. Looking back I should've skipped that but I didn't. I ended up tearing my groin even worse and had to sit out for two months.

About the end of July, I was 50th in the world standings and just decided that I needed to go to winning at that point if I wanted to make anything happen. The very last "big rodeo" at that time was Cow Palace, the Grand National. That's where the PRCA basically made their cuts, who went on to finals and who kissed their season goodbye.

At that time I was such a long shot, I was about $9,000 out of the Finals. I ended up winning both rounds and skidded into the NFR in 12th. Colby Yates will tell you that I said I wasn't going to waste my time going to little rodeos all over, I was basically going to go big or go home. I said I was just going to go to the Cow Palace and "kick the door down" and have that be it.

They were talking me up before I rode and the announcer said, "This cowboy has to win first, he has no other option". He just keeps going on and on. I remember that I was the last bull rider to go and as soon as I stepped off my bull I threw my hat in the air and went to hollering.

As soon as I stepped off that bull it seemed like there was a camera in my face and I had to give an interview. I'm still wearing all my gear and trying to catch my breath. The reporter is asking if I've told anyone yet or how did my family feel about this win. I'm just sucking wind and they hand me a phone and are like, "Why don't you just call you folks right now live on air?"

So I dialed up my parents' house and my dad answered the phone. He was sitting on pins and needles back at the house because he knew what time it was and what was going on. He'd competed back in the day, but never had the opportunity to chase it like I did so he was just a nervous wreck. He answered the phone and said, "Well, what happened?"

I guess it was ESPN that was filming it but they have it all on tape somewhere. I'm telling my dad I rode my bull, I won Cow Palace, and I was headed to the NFR. I was so choked up and about to cry there on live TV, and I think my dad was about the same on the other end of the line.

They turned the cameras off after that and told me thank you for my time. I turned around and went back to get my gear bag. It was like everybody in San Francisco disappeared, the building was completely empty. None of my friends were there, the stands were empty, and I'm just sitting there with my stuff on the fence. It was so quiet I swore I could hear the big, fluorescent lights buzzing.

There were so many emotions going through my mind, I hadn't even really had time to process what all had just happened. I probably hadn't slept a full nights rest in two or three days and it seemed that all that exhaustion and emotion just hit me at once.

I plopped down with my gear bag and just sat there. I was just looking around thinking, "I'm in San Francisco, I'm by myself, I just won Cow Palace, I'm going to the National Finals….". It seemed like my brain was going 900 mph while everything else around me seemed to have just come to a complete standstill.

I'd flown out there by myself; Philip and Colby had already made the NFR so they'd stayed home this time. I just decided to sit there awhile. My rental car was in the parking lot and I wasn't in a big hurry, so why not? I probably sat there for an hour just reflecting on my life, the injuries I'd sustained to get here and how hard I'd worked for it. It all seemed so surreal and I guess I just needed to sit there while it sank in; that I'd accomplished this goal that at one point had seemed so unattainable. I was going to the National Finals Rodeo. I didn't even call anybody. I just sat there.

Before I went back to the rental car I called Philip Elkins. The way things had come down that night I knew he'd gotten bumped out of the NFR by one spot. I thought it was best to call him and tell him myself. He asked how it went and I just really politely said, "Man, I'm sorry, but you're not headed to the NFR." He hung up on me and I don't think we talked for a couple months after that. I felt terrible about it but that's just the sport.

After that I picked my bag up, went to the rental car, and went and sat in traffic for another hour. I didn't even mind the traffic. I just kept replaying it all over in my head. A part of me didn't want the traffic to end because I just wanted to hold onto the moment and the win as long as possible. It was just such a long shot to come back from the bottom and have it all come together like it had.

From that point on, throughout my whole career, nothing else ever came close to that moment. Nothing ever matched that level of an emotional experience. I can still put myself back there and still feel it. I see younger guys chasing the Finals now, all the pressure and it coming down to the wire. I just hope that there's one guy who gets to have that experience and feel that level of elation about making it to the NFR.

People look back and they'll point out this ride or that win in my career, sometimes I don't even remember them. Winning Cow Palace was just the win of a lifetime for me. It is probably the moment I value most in my entire career. Nothing else has ever matched that feeling or that moment.

The very next year I was coming back from a broken arm. I'd broken it in the spring and had been out for a couple months; same circumstances all over again.

Comes to the last rodeo of the year, which was now Dallas. I managed to qualify for it, which was a good thing because it was my hometown and I'd missed it the year before because of injuries.

At this point I had the confidence I could go in there and win so I didn't even enter any rodeos the last two weeks of the season. I was out of the NFR by about $5,000 and I wasn't even worried about it. I knew I had to go into Dallas, ride my bulls, win, and go to the NFR. I was walking around with my chest blown out, it was my hometown and I made sure everyone knew I intended to win it.

I ended up being high 80s on one bull, 90s on the other bulls, and won something like $28,000; I was back in the top 15 then I was headed to the NFR. I broke the arena record with a 95 in front of my hometown and my whole family was in the stands. That was a heck of a feeling!

Just like I remember the feeling at Cow Palace, I remember the feeling in Dallas. It wasn't as overwhelming, but during my victory lap I felt invincible. That was the most confident I had ever felt. I just couldn't be touched. In that moment I swore there wasn't a bull on the planet I couldn't ride.

Those two wins were very different emotionally, but I can put myself back in each moment and it stills gets me. Throughout everything I ever accomplished, those two wins will always mean more to me than any of the others.

Tanner Keeler Aus

Tanner Keeler Aus hails from Granite Falls, Minnesota. When Tanner's dad retired from the sport, Tanner decided to fill his shoes and picked up bareback riding in 1998.
It turned out that riding bareback horses came naturally to the Minnesota cowboy and Tanner was crowned the 2012 College National Champion.

Although he was out most of 2013 with an injury, Tanner has returned to the world of rodeo filled with dedication and determination. He's healthy and happy to be back involved in the sport of rodeo and has big plans for his future.

When he's not on the road Tanner loved to hunt and spend time with his family.

"Free Wi-Fi (With A Side Of Waffles)"

When Ty Breuer and I started traveling together we were broke, really broke. It's certainly not uncommon for a cowboy to have financial struggles, but we were just starting out and it was rough. Every guy has to deal with those "rookie growing pains" though, it's just part of it.

Ty and I decided we needed to find ways to save as much money as possible and in turn not spend money if we could help it. That being said, we went an entire summer without buying a hotel room. We were both rookies and we were traveling around in my van so we decided to make the best of things.

We'd head out on the road, driving from one rodeo to the next. Ty and I would take turns driving until we were both just exhausted. Then we'd find the nicest hotel we could find, and we'd park in a good spot in the corner of their parking lot, and crash there.

We'd use the hotel's Wi-Fi to entertain ourselves; sometimes we had to go to the front desk to ask for the password. I'm surprised no one ever caught on to the fact we'd never checked in to the hotel in the first place. So we'd park close enough to use the free Wi-Fi and if they had a pool we'd have a "pool shower". Chlorine is a good way to kill germs right?

Anyways, in the mornings we'd wake up and walk inside the hotel like we owned the place, like we were staying there and knew exactly where we were going. We'd help ourselves to the continental breakfast bar and maybe sneak some stuff back to the van for later.

After a long rodeo season of sleeping in the van and basically robbing hotels for their amenities, we decided that we'd outgrown that stage of our lives and actually started paying for hotels rooms (thankfully). The hotels might not be as nice, but free waffles are still free waffles.

Skip Ransom

Bull rider Skip Ransom is from Grand Junction, Colorado. Skip was raised on a ranch and started riding calves and steers when he was six.

Skip was slowly progressing up the professional ranks when he made the decision to join the United States Army in October of 2012. Skip's time in the Army will come to an end in 2015 and he'll once again return to the sport of bull riding.

Skip spends any free time he might have at the gym.

"Bulls and Bullets"

I think there are more similarities between bull riding and being in the military than people realize. These are two things that you might not think have a lot in common but they ultimately do. I knew some pretty good people who didn't come home and hear "thank you", who didn't get to come home and kiss their wives, or tell their babies goodnight. When people tell me "thank you" I feel like I don't deserve the thank you because I have the opportunity everyday to wake up and live a life that I love. When people tell me "thank you" I tell them they're welcome, but I don't act like it's a big deal. I think that correlates pretty well into riding bulls.

Riding bulls is a master game of emotions. If you can keep your emotions in check, keep control of your emotions, and take the fear that you have and use it as motivation and drive, then that's the guy that comes out on top. There's a bunch of guys that have ridden bulls before me, won world titles, and just done great things in the sport of bull riding. I don't know too many guys that have been a solider in-between trying to win a world title and then gone back and actually won that world title. I want to be that person.

Being a bull rider prior to joining the Army helped me learn to keep my emotions in check, at least somewhat. When bullets are flying, people are screaming, it's loud, hard to hear, and you're stressed out the worst thing you can do is freak out and lose your mind. When a bull is turning back and you're getting out of shape, getting your chin lifted up or whatever it might be that's getting you out of shape, the worst thing you can do is lose your mind.

Both of those things, being a soldier and a bull rider, have taught me that controlling my emotions and staying mentally stable throughout the event leads to a victory. Now that's not saying that guys like that don't get bucked off, they do, but you can bounce back from it faster. Soldiers possess a super, super, super good ability to pay attention to detail and to control their emotions. The amount of time and training invested in those two things is unbelievable. Soldiers still get shot though, soldiers still die, and bad things still happen. The people who can use their training most consistently though are the ones who come out alive or who can win the event.

I think that's how being in the military has helped me be a better bull rider and vise versa. My being a bull rider definitely helped me be a better soldier. The military forces you to be in shape and to be a bull rider today you have to be an athlete. You can't be a world champion or an aggressive competitor when you're not physically and mentally on the top of your game. You have to have a level of discipline and you have to be an athlete.

"Grow Up, Kid"

I had just turned 17 and it was the summer before my senior year of high school. I was riding bulls really, really hot. I'd probably been to 50 rodeos and maybe got bucked off three or four bulls. I had just moved up from Juniors to Open and I was making money and enjoying it. I was probably enjoying too much of the wrong stuff too, but I was young and didn't know better.

I'd left a bull riding in Fayetteville, PA and I was on my way to another one in West Virginia. I had borrowed my uncle's 1992 single cab, 5-speed Ford Ranger. I was honestly too tired and sleepy to be driving. I was just not going to stop though. I was really "gung ho" about going to a bull riding every weekend and a lack of sleep wasn't going to prevent that. I didn't care how I got there or how fast I got there, I was going.

So there was this gravel road that I knew you could use as a cut through, it was kind of something only people who traveled up and down the road a lot knew about. It was kind of steep and there was a sharp turn at the end. I was listening to my Chris LeDoux and I was just driving, until I fell asleep. I went around that corner and hit the pavement and the jolt was enough to wake me up. I overcorrected and went off about a 20-25' embankment into a creek bed, ended nose down, and bent the frame all up.

I'd hit my head on the steering wheel and cracked my knee on the dashboard. I'd opened up the door but was still kind of out of it. I fell out of the truck about 10' and ended up landing on a rock and bruising my hip pretty badly. I called my dad and called my uncle, told them all what happened, and they came and got me.

I then called my Uncle Doug. My cousin DJ and I were both currently living with him and we were both going to this bull riding in West Virginia. They were headed down there as well so we met them and the three of us trucked on down to West Virginia.

I ended up making the short round at this bull riding. My knee was twice the size it should have been, my head was killing me, and I was having double vision, but I made the decision that I was still going to ride in the short round. Matt DeShon had a bull that he'd just bought from Chad Berger and this bull had been to the PBR Build Ford Tough Series about three months prior to this. This bull was a rank sucker, just no joke, and I drew him in the short round. Even though I'd gotten in this wreck four hours prior I felt invincible.

Well in one jump he'd jerked me down over my hand and I was in the mud. I got up and went behind the bucking chutes and in my hazy state things just dawned on me. I was like, "Alright God, I got it. I'm human. I understand." I realized I still needed to act like a bull rider who was hungry, a bull rider who had a negative bank account. I wasn't a world champion and I needed to stop acting like it.

That's probably the event when I stopped drinking and started taking things seriously. I realized I needed to grow up, hit the gym, and focus more on the right things than the wrong things.

"Losing Your Lunch"

My senior year of high school we went to the National Farm Show in Pennsylvania. It's one of the largest high school rodeos in the country; attendance is usually about 8,000 people per performance, with two performances a day. It's a big deal. I was a student president so people knew who I was and were paying attention to what I did both in the arena and out of it. I had just turned 18 and had my PBR permit. The people who really knew me knew that I'd been going to some PBR events and they were really excited to see what I was going to do in my senior year of high school.

Before we'd headed up there, I knew I'd drawn this little brown bull, Scarface. He was a cool looking bull with almost a white lightning strike on his face. He was a good bull too; I knew he was going to go to the left and really up and down. I ride left-handed so it was right in my wheelhouse and I was just ready to get there and win it.

Well right before the NFS I got the flu. I mean I got the flu BAD. I was so sick, like couldn't even keep water down sick. But I knew I'd drawn this bull and I was going to ride him no matter what. So we head up there, which felt like the longest trip of my life, and I get ready to ride this bull. I was the last guy out in the first round. There are 8,000 people in the stands all looking at you so you'd better not blow it, you know?

He went out there one jump and went back to the left. I have a curse, or whatever you want to call it, if a bull goes into my hand, he's getting spurred. I started spurring him and it felt so amazing. For 7.5 seconds it was the prettiest, nicest, smoothest high school bull ride you'd probably ever seen.

At about 7.5 seconds I got really sick and threw up on the back of this bull. I was wearing a helmet at the time; I had like a clear shield on mine versus the new metal wire design. So my helmet is filled with vomit, it's getting in my eyes, going up my noise, more is coming out, it was a disaster and everyone was oblivious to it but me.

Needless to say I ended up getting bucked off. They thought I'd ridden at first, but on the replay they'd decided I hadn't. I asked the judges what they'd marked that bull and me, since I had originally had a score and all. I was 87.5 at a high school rodeo and the highest marked ride that year was an 83. So not only did I lose a buckle but I lost my lunch as well.

The next round I was still sick as a dog but still determined to compete no matter what. I slept all afternoon and dragged myself to the arena. I was in the last section of the bulls; I'd drawn this big black bull, Black Bart. I'd never turned out a bull in my life and wasn't about to start, so I climbed on and braced for one more ride. He made about two jumps and for lack of a better term, I had a bit of an explosion in my pants on the back of him. Realizing what I'd done I just got off of him, grabbed my rope, and walked back behind the chutes with a crap load in my pants.

My dad was back there and I just looked at him and went, "Dad, I have shit myself, I have thrown up on myself, and I still didn't win a buckle. I think I'm done. Can we go home now?" We ended up going to the hospital after the rodeo. I was so sick my kidney function was at like 20%. I knew I was sick, but I didn't really know how sick. My body just didn't have any fluid left in it. I'd done two rounds of calf roping, two rounds of team roping, and ridden two bulls and I hadn't been able to drink or eat for 16 hours.

That's probably my most embarrassing moment as a bull rider. I can't say I'd ever done that before or have done it since.

"Like Lane"

My mom and dad were in Cheyenne in July of 1989, when Lane Frost passed away. At the time my mom just happened to be pregnant with me. They were headed to the arena but my mom started cramping so they headed to the hospital instead. Lane died about the time they got to the hospital. From the minute they'd announced that Lane Frost had died, I didn't move, kick, nothing inside my mom for 24 hours. I was completely, perfectly still.

Time marches on, and I was born in December of that year. Fast-forward to 1992 when the PBR was first televised. I remember this like it was yesterday. People say you can't remember anything when you're two years old, but I remember this. I was sitting on the living room floor with my dad. I had one of those toys that was a horse on springs you bounce up and down on, only I had a bull. I had my little chaps on, my underwear, and my cowboy hat and I was just riding the heck out of this thing. I turned to my dad and told him I was going to be a world champion bull rider; he just laughed because I was three years old. From that point on though I was infatuated with the sport.

We'd go to local rodeos and I was always all about the bull riding. When I was six we went to the Delta County fair in Colorado and I wanted to be in the calf riding. My dad was like, "No way, you mother would kill me, no way." I was just pestering him about it and he kept saying no. I ended up throwing the biggest fit in the history of fits. I was promising I wouldn't tell mom, kicking and rolling in the dirt, throwing my shoes, just the works.

My poor dad ended up caving in, coughed up $50, and signed me up for the calf riding. I didn't have a helmet, chaps, or glove, but I was going to ride so I climbed on this calf with my Walmart buckle and boots. I ended up winning the calf riding and from that point forward it was just a done deal; no one was going to stop me.

I didn't even know the part about Lane Frost until I was 15 or 16. Before that I'd gone to the National Junior High Finals with my cousin. We'd both qualified to ride out there, so we just went together. We were just walking and laughing and this lady walked by and then came back and stopped me. She looked me square in the eye and said, "You remind me so much of Lane Frost, you have his smile."

Lane Frost was always, and will always be, one of my biggest idols and heroes, but at that point my mom hadn't told me the story yet. I came home and told her what this lady had said to me and she finally told me about being at Cheyenne the day he died.

A couple years later when I was 22, I was really struggling as a person and with my life. I needed to fix myself and I knew that joining the Army was the only way I was going to get things together. The Army was going to get me back on the right path. During that time I got a lot closer to God and I started having these talks with Lane. I'd say, "Okay Lane, I know you're not happy with me. I know I'm not being the bull rider you'd like to represent your legacy." I was just crying like a baby. I felt so defeated and I felt like I'd let him down almost.

From that day forward, I did a complete 180 with my life. I enjoy my life, but I fill in the dark spots with practice bulls, my faith, and working out. But I lost some time there and I'm ready to fight my way back to the top again. I know I'm capable of being a world champion and I won't stop until I am one.

Paige Stout

Paige Stout is from Weatherford, TX. She was raised in the world of rodeo, more specifically bull riding. Her grandfather was a professional bull rider and her dad was a bullfighter for many years.

At the age of 10 Paige purchased her first bucking bull and began competing with him. It didn't take long for her to realize that her passion was raising and hauling bucking bulls. Growing up she competed in youth futurities. In 2009, she won the title of NBBA Reserve Youth Champion. In 2012, she won the NBBA Bull Bash Youth Champion, as well as ABBI Junior World Champion.

With much heart and dedication she eventually increased her stock and at the first available chance, when she turned 18, Paige hauled bulls to her first Professional Bull Riders Built Ford Tough event in St. Louis, MO. Paige was selected to have one of her bulls buck at the 2014 PBR World Finals and at the 2014 Wrangler National Finals.

Paige now attends and hauls bull to PBR events all across the country. She is also currently attending Weatherford College where she is studying towards her degree in Nursing.

"Dreaming for a Buckle"

At a really young age I grew a passion for raising and hauling bucking bulls. I purchased my first bucking bull at the age of 10 and began competing in youth futurities. It was always a feeling of pure joy and excitement every time one of my bulls bucked, getting to see all of my hard work and dedication being represented in each bull was very rewarding to me. As much as I loved the feeling of flanking my bulls then watching them buck their hearts out from behind the chutes, I was craving something more. I had dreams to win a championship buckle.

I competed in many youth futurities with a lot of different bulls. I came so close to winning that champion buckle on several different occasions. As I grew older and began competing more, the competition was getting tougher. Not to mention the pressure of winning that buckle was building up as I was nearing my last year to be able to compete in the youth futurities, as you had to be 18 or younger.

It was the last youth futurity I ever entered and competed in that had the most impact on my life. It was the American Bucking Bull Incorporated (ABBI) World Finals, which was held in Las Vegas, NV. On the spur of the moment, I decided to enter the ABBI Junior futurity one last time.

No matter what happened in that arena, this event was going to be one of the most fun events I had ever entered. The arena, the atmosphere, and the crowd all made the excitement much more intense. My youth bull, Rim Shot, was the very last one to buck that day. I not so patiently waited behind the chutes, watching every bull before mine perform to the best of their ability, and let me tell you, the bulls brought the heat at this competition! When it was finally my turn for my bull to buck I got him ready in the chute with his flank and nodded my head for the chute gate to open.

Rim Shot bucked better on that day than I have ever seen him. He picked perfect timing to step it up and show us what he was made of. When they put his scores up on the big screen I was grinning ear to ear and couldn't contain my excitement. I knew that performance and score just earned him the title of ABBI Junior World Champion Bucking Bull.

I was so honored and excited that we had won and I was finally getting that gold buckle that I had worked so hard for. Thanks to Rim Shot I proudly wear that champion buckle around my waist.

"Mom's Always Right"

Working with bulls day in and day out you begin to develop a routine. I'm at the point now where I have learned the different personalities of each bull. There are some bulls that are friendlier than others and enjoy having their backs scratched while there are others that are unpredictable and you can't turn your back on. I have also learned that when working with bulls as much as I do, it is not "if you get hurt, but when."

I've had one too many close calls with the bulls, but luckily the majority of them I got away with just minor bumps and bruises. However, there was the one night when I was in routine mode and let my guard down. It's those gut instincts that tell you whether what you're about to do is the right or the wrong choice, but of course on this night I didn't listen to those instincts.

It was a Friday night in November and I already had plans to take several of my bulls to a bull team competition about 30 miles away. As we were trying to load the trailer a bad storm came rolling in and it began to sleet. The roads were already slick, but now they were even more dangerous. This is when my instincts told me to stay home, but I wasn't listening.

After much convincing, I talked my dad into going with me to the bull riding, all the while my mom repeating that something just didn't feel right and it was a bad idea considering the weather conditions. We finished loading and set out for the bull competition. Luckily, the further east we drove the weather eased up and we arrived safely at our destination.

I had some of the first bulls out that night so as usual, I was back behind the chutes getting my bulls ready in the loading pens by hanging the flanks on them. I got the first one ready, no problem. The second bull, however, was a new bull for me that I was trying out for the first time.

He was feeling a little rambunctious. I struggled to get him situated, as he was getting pretty anxious in the loading pen. I just about had his flank tied on him when he really got upset. He kicked through the panels with enough force to knock me off my feet. That exact same instant a feeling came over me that I have felt several times before. I knew something was broken but due to the radiating pain in my entire right leg, I just couldn't tell what bone was broken. I had the bulls exact hoof print right over the top of my knee.

At this point I had already paid entry fees for the bulls to compete so there was no backing out now. Obviously I was in no state to climb behind the back of the chutes and flank, but thankfully I brought dad along! After they carried me to the truck, my dad ran back into the coliseum just in time to flank my bulls. As I sat in the truck by myself waiting I realized that my instincts proved me wrong. That this wasn't going to be a good phone call back home to mom, who was the one telling me this whole thing wasn't a good idea.

My dad filled in for me by flanking the bulls and getting them loaded back in the trailer for the trip back home. By this time, it was dark and the temperatures had dropped below freezing. We fought the wind and the ice all the way home and then to the emergency room. I'm blessed that my parents support me and attend the majority of events where I take bulls, but I'm even more so thankful that my dad was with me that night.

After a long night in the emergency room, I found out the fibula in my lower leg was snapped into two pieces. It was going to be several months of recovery, but the most important lesson I learned that night was that there will be those times when you choose not to follow your gut instinct, but never go against your momma's advice because she is always right!!

"How To Meet Your Neighbors"

Our ranch is in a pretty convenient location to simply use as a meeting place or when stock contractors are traveling long distances and need a place to stop to unload bulls off their trailer for the night. We feel it is important to extend the same courtesy to other stock contractors that have been extended to us when we are on the road and away from home.

We have a friend that was selling a two-year-old bull and needed a place to use as a meeting spot for the buyer to pick up the bull. Without hesitation, we told him to use one of our pens to hold the bull until the buyer arrives. He only needed a pen for the bull for about an hour. This is a pretty common request and something we do frequently. What could possibly go wrong in that short period of time?

On this particular, very, very hot summer day I was at the pens helping the guys move the bull around. The man that had just bought the bull was already backed up and ready to put the bull on his trailer. The bull was already really worked up and being as young as he was, he wasn't quite used to the trailer rides.   After many attempts the bull finally decided to head towards the trailer to load up.   At that exact same moment I realized that when they backed the trailer up to the pens the gate did not get tied to the trailer just in case the bull tried to slip in between and get out. Sure as shootin' that two year old crazy bull wiggled himself in between the trailer and the gate and freed himself to 20 plus acres.

If the bull had stayed within the 20 acres it would have been an easy solution to the problem. However, to make matters a little more difficult, the gate to the entrance of the property was wide open, leading to busy roads and neighborhoods. It's almost like that bull knew exactly where that open entry gate was and he took off for it.

So now I am on foot chasing a bull up and down roads trying to detour him away from going into neighborhoods, while also trying to avoid either of us getting hit by all the traffic in the area. I would get the bull turned around to try and head back to the ranch and then he would get spooked and change his mind and head down another road. I had several people in cars stop to offer me a ride to chase down the bull. I didn't know who any of the people were, they were all strangers to me, so politely and very out of breath I declined their offer and kept running on foot.

We had been entertaining the neighbors and all the passer byers for over an hour by now when the neighbors across the street from our ranch decided to try and help by opening their gate to their backyard. They were just hoping by chance we could corner the bull and he would willingly go into their backyard. Luckily, he decided to check out the green grass in their backyard.

Half the battle was now over. We officially got to meet our neighbors for the first time. This was not exactly the introduction we had envisioned, but nonetheless they were very friendly considering they now had a nervous bull penned up in their backyard with no way to get him loaded on a trailer to take him back to the ranch.

As the sun began to set we knew we were running out of daylight and we would have to wait till morning to get the bull loaded. Before it got too dark to see, we decided to go back to our ranch and bring over my mini bull, "Furby", to keep the bull company and to hopefully get him to calm down, and make the process go a littler smoother in the morning.

Our neighbors now had two new backyard "pets" for the evening. They were so nice about the whole situation by offering to let the bulls stay in their backyard until the next morning. We were hoping they wouldn't change their mind in the middle of the night and decide to open their gate and let them out when they realized they now had two bulls in their perfectly manicured yard.

The next morning was spent building a makeshift pen that we could use to persuade the bulls to go into so we wouldn't tear up the neighbors yard driving the truck and trailer through it. With a lot of patience and persistence, loading the bulls was finally a success.

This experience taught me that not only to tie *every* gate, but also that I am not in shape to be chasing bulls down back roads!

Thad Newell

Thad Newell was born and raised in Bristow, Oklahoma. Thad grew up around rodeo and naturally fell into the sport of bull riding, propelling him towards successful careers in the PRCA and currently in the PBR.

Thad is an 8x BRI event champion and was the 2013 Don Gay Bull Riding Tour Finals Champion.

Thad will be featured in an upcoming documentary "Surfer Cowboy", produced by Bryan Jennings for the non-profit organization Walking on Water.

When he isn't riding bulls Thad spends his time hunting, fishing, roping, training horses, and spending as much time as he can with his son.

"Encounters"

It's pretty common knowledge in the rodeo world that buckle bunnies are a prominent thing and man, a few of my buddies have really gotten themselves in trouble when it comes to that. I keep away from that stuff now that I've grown up and I'm a dad, but I was young once just like everyone else.

One time my buddies and I were in Carney, Nebraska at a bull riding; we'll just call these guys Maverick and Goose. We went to the local bar that everyone gravitated towards after the bull riding and decided to have ourselves a good time. We're just drinking beers and giving each other hell about our rides. As we're doing this Maverick is getting pretty well trashed.

After a couple hours Goose and I realize Maverick is missing; he'd just disappeared and left us. We went out to the parking lot and the truck was gone. Man, Goose and I were steaming. We're blowing up his phone and he's not answering. We realized we're going to have to walk back to the hotel at this point, and it's not just next-door.

It's pouring rain in Carney and Goose and I hiked about five miles back to the hotel. Needless to say we were stone cold sober and pretty ticked off by the time we got there. We headed straight to Maverick's room because we honestly wanted to whoop his ass for leaving us.

We go to pounding on the door and surprise, Maverick answers.

Except Maverick answered the door still pretty drunk and butt naked. Apparently he'd taken a girl home from the bar and she'd passed out before they could get to mattress dancing. He looked like a 16-year-old boy who might cry and let's just say things were "hard" on him when he answered the door.

Goose and I just dissolved with laughter. We stumbled back into the hallway and were almost at the point of tears we were laughing so hard. We just looked at each other and went, "Poor guy." Goose and I just went back to our room and the next morning we just didn't even bring it up. I think Maverick was pretty embarrassed about it and we just couldn't stop chuckling.

Another time we were in a similar situation with another friend that we'll just call Iceman. Same old story, Goose, Iceman, and I had all gone to a bull riding and Iceman had decided to take this girl back to the room with him. They did exactly what you'd expect, but the next morning Iceman got a little bit of a surprise.

Iceman had taken home a one-handed hooker. This chick was completely missing a hand and he didn't even notice until the morning after. He's never living that one down, that's for sure.

I tried to keep myself out of situations like that but I can't say I didn't enjoy poking fun at my friends when they found themselves in the middle of some unfortunate encounters.

"Just A Lil' Broken"

One time, when I was still in the PRCA, I was like #2 in rankings and I had torn my shoulder all to hell. It'd been building over a couple rodeos and I couldn't even get it to stay in the socket. Tandy Freeman, Justin Sports Medicine's Orthopedic Specialist, said we needed to address it ASAP, so I had surgery and he put eight anchors in my shoulder to hold it in place. After I healed up from that I went back to riding again and I'd worked my way back up into the Top 10 again. It was about mid-season so I felt pretty confident with how things were going again and I thought the NFR was a definite possibility.

I went to Gladewater, TX and at that time I was sitting pretty up there in the standings, easily in the Top 10. We went to one of Don Gay's rodeos and it had just poured the night before. The arena was really muddy. I got this bull that was supposedly a handful, it was either no one had ridden him or he was just really rank. Either way, I decided I wanted to make a point to really spur him.

We go out and just as I go to spurring him, right towards the end of the 8 seconds, he slips in the mud. He basically flipped and whipped me down in front of him and I landed on my hands and knees. The bullfighter came in to distract him and when he did, the bull turned and brought both his hind feet down right square on my back. He flattened me out like a pancake, I'm pretty sure he stomped all the oxygen out of my body.

I ended up popping my shoulder out of the socket and breaking it; popped my hip out and broke it too. I knew it was bad when I couldn't move to get away, I couldn't even crawl. I've been hurt a lot but usually I have been able to get out of the arena or at least crawl into a chute and get away. I tried to prop myself up on my arms and hips to like army crawl and couldn't move; my whole right side wouldn't work. One of the bullfighters realized I wasn't moving and kind of picked me up and tossed me in a chute until they got the bull out of the arena.

That took me out of action for about a year, and my hip still isn't right. I was supposed to have surgery on it and the morning of my surgery they came in and told me the doctor had decided I was too young to have the surgery. I was so mad, I'd been in the hospital all night and they just sprung it on me. I hadn't been able to eat or drink for like 12 hours and then they decided not to do the surgery at all. I can't spur one like I used to. I used to be able to bring my knee almost up to my jawline or my ear and I just can't do that anymore. It gets stiff pretty easily so I decided to go to the PBR and give that a shot before I was too old and banged up to ride anymore. The first PBR event I went to I was 90.5 and won the long round. I was marked to be 94 in the short round and he bucked me off at 7.9. I managed to make the cut anyways, but I decided I needed to go to just one more event.

I headed to Pensacola, FL and drew a bull I'm pretty sure wasn't even supposed to be there. He was so small my rope didn't even fit him. It was pretty ridiculous. I'm surprised my toes didn't touch the arena floor on him. Well he went out and the ride wasn't bad at all at first, then he spotted one of the bullfighters and so he clicked my heels and I got hung up. He pulled this funny move and I'm long-legged on this little bitty thing.

Whenever it hung me up he went to turn and just stepped square on my knee, it blew everything out. I didn't have a knee left at all so they went in and replaced my knee with a cadaver's knee. Tandy said if it had turned another half inch or something they would've had to take my leg off from the knee down because it would've busted the main artery in my leg.

So I get a whole new knee and my body starts rejecting part of it; my PCL didn't take so I still don't have a PCL in my knee. I have to wear a brace to ride and it definitely affects me. Here again, I have to just find a way to work around it and do the best I can with what I've got left.

In April of 2014 I headed to the PBR DeWALT Guaranteed Tough Invitational in Nampa, Idaho. I drew a bull called "Prince Albert". He had a lot of momentum and ended up getting my feet loose and behind me. So I bucked off at like 5 seconds but on the way down he hooked me twice in the shoulder, really hard back-to-back blows. I ended up breaking my shoulder blade and was out for even more time.

October of 2014 I decided to go down the road to my buddies "Give Cancer The Boot" benefit bull riding event. I figured it'd be a good way to get some practice and put some money in the bank. It was right down the road from my house so I just thought it'd be an easy deal for me; things didn't really work out that way. I drew a bull that I do not like at all. I went to get off of him away from my hand and as I was going to get off I hung my spur up, like way up by my handle.

Because I'm so long legged it just hung me right there under his back feet. He stomped on me about four or five times, ripped the bottom of my right ear off, then stomped on my jaw really good. I had to get 30 some stitches between my ear and my face, and I broke two teeth. I was conscious throughout the whole thing.

A day or two later someone sent me a video of the whole thing. Watching that video just put it all into perspective for me; it could have been way worse than it was. I was lucky to be sitting there even watching the video. If I'd had a helmet on, the way he stepped on my face, it could have twisted my neck and broken it. It was not the easy event I was expecting that's for sure.

That's part of bull riding though; no way you're going to get through it without getting hurt, I just seemed to have compounded all my injuries into a condensed period of time. It's not stopping me anytime soon though.

Jarrett Blessing

Jarrett Blessing is a steer roper from Paradise, Texas. Jarrett is a middle school agriculture/industrial technology teacher, which prevents him from competing as intensely as he used to.

Jarrett joined the PRCA in 2002. Jarrett qualified for the National Finals Steer Roping three times (2002, 2005, 2007), and also won the NFSR average title in 2007.

When he's not competing or teaching Jarrett happily spends time with his wife and two kids.

"Sixteenth"

2014 started off pretty slow. I was just going to season my new horse, take my family on vacation, and rope a little bit. My horse was really green so I didn't think I had a real good chance at making the Finals. I figured I'd just get him working more and leave it at that. I went to some rodeos in the spring and did okay. When summer comes around and I missed a lot of rodeos because I either didn't enter, I was in school training for my job, or stuff just came up.

I was going to take this young horse to some rodeos; just to get him some more experience and work on building his confidence. I was going to a few rodeos before Cheyenne Frontier Days so I might have a shot at Cheyenne. The first rodeo we went to in Woodward, Oklahoma, they ended up cancelling it because they couldn't get steers. That was a blow because I was really counting on that one to help me let this horse have a shot at a decent run and really build up his confidence. It was just all slack and not a performance, lots of practice, but then they cancelled it.

Then I entered another little Oklahoma rodeo, the first rodeo we end up going to with a full-on performance. First run he does great but I'm way too long and don't win anything. Second run I drew a steer that was so-so. I figured I'd just make a solid run, tie the steer, let my horse get used to the crowd, just anything to build some confidence in my young horse. I ended up making a really decent run and won some money but my horse really struggled, he has turned around and was pretty jumpy. I'd won some money but wasn't pleased with how my horse had run.

I went home for about three days to try and focus a bit before Cheyenne. I had this other horse at home that I trip steers on, but I'd given him to my wife. He'd gotten hurt a couple times or it seemed like every time I'd haul him he'd do great for a little bit and then he'd get sore. I'd gotten so frustrated with things that I'd just given him to my wife. I swore I wasn't going to ride him anymore and he could stay sound for what she wanted to do.

Well after my green horse hadn't done well I came home and told my wife I was going to borrow her horse and tie some steers on him to see how he did. He's always worked well, but I just couldn't keep him sound long term. I knew I couldn't ride my green horse in Cheyenne and I wouldn't have a chance at all if I did. I tied one steer down and logged him a bit and this horse worked phenomenally. I decided to take him to Cheyenne so I'd have a fighting chance at winning something.

So off we go to Cheyenne and I placed in the 1st round, won 2nd in the short, won the average, won like $15,00. I hadn't even been going to that many rodeos so it bumped me from about 30th to 9th in the world. I'd just borrowed my wife's horse for one rodeo and it had changed the whole game!

I didn't enter that many rodeos after Cheyenne. You're supposed to enter all these rodeos so if you do well at Cheyenne you'll be entered elsewhere so you can really clinch your NFR spot; I'd only entered Deadwood and Lovington. So I went to Deadwood, which is during Cheyenne, rode my green horse and he did mediocre. I didn't win anything. Went back to Cheyenne, won that, and then I realized after Cheyenne I needed to hustle and enter a bunch of places because my shot at making the NFR was pretty real.

I was entered in Lovington, but teacher training was starting right after that so I missed like six or seven rodeos because of the training. I hadn't really entered anything after Cheyenne, because I'd never really expected to be in the position to make the Finals in the first place. I ended up missing about a dozen rodeos between Cheyenne and when I started being able to enter again after school started.

I headed up to the Northeast for Ellensburg, Walla Walla, Lewiston, and Pendleton. I placed at Ellensburg and missed my steer in the short round at Pendleton. I don't miss steers often, if anything I like the pressure of performing when there's a lot on the line. I usually rise to that occasion and perform even better; I just popped it off my steer to win third in the short round.

I spent a bunch of money flying back and forth up there too. Flew to Ellensburg, went to Walla Walla and Lewiston, flew home and taught for a week, then flew to Pendleton and roped Monday and Tuesday in the slack. From there I flew back home and taught Wednesday, Thursday, and Friday, flew back to Pendleton that weekend for the short round and ended up missing my steer. I ended up placing 7th. Luckily I'd won a round. I was still in the top 15, but there were guys right on my heels in the standings.

I flew back home and went to Amarillo and Apache. I didn't draw very well and just didn't have any luck. I'm still riding my wife's good horse and he's trying his best but things just weren't working in our favor. So it comes down to the rodeo in Stephenville and it's the last rodeo of the year. I'm $560 behind Troy Tillard and he's having just as much heck at these other rodeos as I am.

It comes down to this last rodeo. My first steer, I tie down but don't place and my second steer just stopped and my rope popped off. Troy ended up drawing that same steer for his third run and his run went about the same as mine had. The steer stopped just like it had with me. So it comes down to the last steer for us both at the last rodeo of the season to determine who's going to finals and who isn't. I was sitting there calculating and I knew if I split 4th/5th I'd be good, make up the $560, and make the NFR.

When I roped 11.6 was winning fourth and there were still solid ropers after me. I figured I needed to be 11.1, which was winning third at the time. My game plan was to go as fast as I could and not make mistakes. I go out there and roped really aggressively and ended up being 10.7. I ran back to my horse and I'm just flying high, I've cinched the NFR. That run felt so smooth and easy; my horse was on point, and it just felt awesome. The crowd is just going nuts and I felt incredible.

My steer kicked loose before the six seconds were up. I'd gone from being on top of the world to missing the NFR in about 2 seconds, all because this steer kicked loose.

What was ironic about it is that Troy Tillard, who did make the NFR, called me a couple days later because he'd watched that 10.7 run and had left the arena before he knew my steer got up. He'd thought he'd missed the Finals based on that run so he kind of had a clue how devastated I felt. Finishing 16th sucked, it just did. You just go over all the little mistakes over the year and you see where you should have done better or should've done something different. If I'd known it was going to come down to $560 I would've saved my green horse and just tried to ride my good horse all season long.

Finishing 16th is just rough, to be that close and miss it. If I was younger and I'd never made the Finals it would have been even more devastating. I think if I'd been really working hard all season to make it, and not missed rodeos because of school, that would have made it even harder. The best thing to come out of it is that my good horse, which I'd given to my wife, is sound now. He never got sore. I took him to easily ten rodeos in a row and he just felt great at every one. It's not necessarily good for my wife but it's good for me. I told someone the other day that someone needed to write a song about being 16th. There are a lot of people who are 16th every year, and let me tell you it's not easy being 16th. Guys who are 16th try to forget it even happened. I think unless you've been there you can't really grasp how bad it feels. If you're one of those guys who have busted their butt all year long trying to make it to every rodeo, only to miss out by one spot is really hard to swallow.

I'm really glad I won Cheyenne because that's something I've always wanted to do. It all just came together, and it was definitely one of my highest highs. My lowest low came just shortly after that.

That's rodeo though, one second things and are amazing and you feel on top of the world, then two seconds later all that can change.

Justin Scofield

Justin Scofield is a team roper that hails from Flandreau, South Dakota. Justin credits doing every day work on his grandfather's ranch as the motivator for getting him involved in the sport of rodeo; Justin's parents steered him in the direction of tie-down roping versus roughstock events.

Justin has been roping professionally for 16 years and he bought his PRCA card in 1998.
Justin has a couple young horses in the works so for now he's focused on circuit rodeos.

When he's not competing Justin is training horses and working for Hande Equine Therapy in Dickinson, North Dakota helping with their equine swimming program.
In his spare time Justin like to hunt and spend time with friends.

"Highs and Lows"

Rodeo and roping just takes you all over, and without a doubt one of my favorite rodeos is Cheyenne Frontier Days. I've been roping and competing a long time and nothing ever compares to that arena and that rodeo.

Cheyenne is just anybody's game. If you draw one that's good and wants to let you win then you might have a shot. I've competed there quite a few times and I've never gotten lucky enough to win it, but it hasn't kept me from going back and trying again and again. I was one spot out of making the short round one year and I still want that short round spot.

The first time you go to Cheyenne is pretty special. You always hear things about it but experiencing it for the first time is eye opening. It's a massive rodeo with the best livestock; it's just different from anything else. It's just neat because it's more of the cowboy atmosphere. You can see guys win there who you might have never heard of. It's a giant lottery and it's anybody's game.

The atmosphere is probably what makes Cheyenne so unique. It's just huge and I don't think people who've never been there can really grasp that. During the slack there are still tons of people packed in the stands to watch, it's just a special place.

Another rodeo that matters to me is the National Western in Denver; I was lucky enough to win that in 2006. I went through the qualifier deal and the rodeo was just so smooth. It was a life-changing deal for me. Winning the National Western just set me up to rodeo a lot that year and it just kick-started my whole season.

One year I'd been going to circuit rodeos all year and it'd just been miserable. I hadn't won anything and wasn't having any luck. All of sudden during the fall, I started winning everything; that's the best feeling in the world. I was on such a roll and winning almost felt easy. I finally felt like things had turned around. My horse was performing well, and there's just no feeling like winning. That's rodeo though; one month you're at the bottom of the barrel and the next month you feel like you're effortlessly winning everything.

I've always tried to finish my horses myself. It takes three to four years to just season them, so it's not the most time-effective way to go about things. When I train my own though, I know what I'm sitting on and I feel like I have a better understanding of what they're capable of. Usually I rodeo on young horses, get them going, and sell them. That's how rodeo becomes more of a business for me than just a sport or a competition. I love winning, I do, but when I can win and then make money selling roping horses, it doesn't get much more rewarding than that.

The horse makes the roper, there's no doubt about that. You can put a really good roper on a mediocre horse and get a mediocre roper, but if you put a good roper on a good horse then you'll have a good roper. You have to know the horse that you back into the box, know when they deliver a peak performance, when they're not right, or when they don't love it.

You just have to get those young horses as much exposure as you can; indoor rodeos, outdoor rodeos, big crowds, small crowds. You just have to make sure you cover all your bases. If you do get a horse that doesn't take to roping, then you just have to find the event or career they want to do. If a horse loves his job, then he'll excel at it. When people come up and tell you that your horse works well though, that's pretty neat. You feel like you've really accomplished something when people compliment you on them or really bug you to sell them.

Rodeo is hard though, and roping is hard. People need to realize that sometimes we put 80,000 miles on a truck in a few months or a year just going from rodeo to rodeo. It's fun and no matter what, I can't seem to give it up. It's hard to really make a decent living doing rodeo; some can but most can't. You can go to a sale and pick out a young horse that should be a champion and sometimes things don't work out that way; a horse can be bred to perform and end up being a dud. That's just part of the ups and downs of rodeo. Nothing's guaranteed.

You just have to make sure you hang around the people who are winning and who are positive, because those are the people you're going to learn the most from and they're going to help you the most. If everybody in the truck is positive and the atmosphere is positive, winning is way easier under those circumstances. You have to travel with people you trust and who will pick you up when you have a bad run.

I've always said a bad day of roping is better than a good day of work. It's fun and you've got to love it. So long as I feel competitive, I'll keep doing it. I guess the day might come when I don't feel competitive anymore, but I don't see that happening anytime soon. When a kid stops you and asks for advice though, that's when you feel like all your hard work and the hours on the road are paying off. Just to know that someone is looking up to you makes you feel like it's worth it.

Heath Ford

Heath Ford was born and raised in Greeley, CO but now calls Slocum, TX home.
Heath has been to the NFR three times (2006, 2007, 2009) and is currently a PRCA board member and bareback riding representative.

Heath has been going to professional rodeos since 1996 and has qualified for the circuit finals 17 times.

When he's not on the road Heath enjoys taking care of his ranch, hunting, fishing, and enjoying time with his family, his wife Brittney, and their daughter. Heath is also an ordained minister; he always enjoys the opportunity to preach when he can.

"Healed"

In 2010 I was at a rodeo in Red Bluff, CA. That was the year I started dating the gal who would become my wife, and she was going to school in Dillon, Montana at the time. So I took off to go to Red Bluff and it had poured rain there the day before the rodeo. To dry the arena they'd brought in a bunch of helicopters to hover over the arena to dry the dirt out. When they came back in and worked the arena dirt it made like little hard pebbles, almost like a pea-gravel.

I got on my horse and rode no problem, heard the buzzer, and told the pickup man I was coming to him. Just as I reached for him his horse kind of shied away from me. His horse went one way and my horse went the other. It made a pretty big space between us and I couldn't close the gap. I thought, "Well, you're going to crash here pretty good and you're probably going to get run over by that other pickup man's horse." I figured if I landed on my feet and just kept moving I might be okay.

I jumped off and landed on my feet but that pebble-dirt wasn't steady and it made my feet slide out from under me. I came down hard and ended up landing with my butt right between my ankle and my knee and broke my leg. I sat out there and kept trying to get up but I could feel something wasn't right. I kind of worked myself over by the fence and kept trying to talk myself into getting up.

They go to bucking another horse and I just knew he was going to come over there and run me over, so I tried to crawl underneath the fence. Some guy grabbed me and drug me out of the arena. He said they were about to run a race and I needed to get out of there. About that time six horses come flying around the track and I was trying to get out of the arena, up a fence, and away from these horses on the track. I just couldn't move.

I don't think anybody realized I was actually hurt, but my brother came out to help me and I told him I was pretty sure my leg was broken. We get out of the arena and he helped me get to the Justin Sports Medicine trailer. There was a cowboy preacher in the trailer and he asked me what was injured. I explained to him they thought my leg was broken and I was headed to get x-rays done. He prayed for God to realign my bones and make my leg new again and then we prayed together about it real quick.

I went to the doctor, got my x-rays, and you could see the clean break on the x-rays. At this point in time though my leg was fairly swollen and they didn't want to do anything until the swelling went down. They told me to keep it elevated and iced for about a week then we'd take new x-rays and see if I needed surgery or if just a cast would do. My leg was just too swollen for them to do anything at the moment.

I called Brittney up in Montana and told her I was just going to come crash on her couch for a week. I'd had a flight to go back to some other rodeo but clearly I wasn't going to be up to that. I told her I was just going to come hang out with her; I didn't know what else to do. So for a week I crashed on her and her roommate's couch and kept my leg iced and elevated just like they told me. Brittney and I would pray over my leg a couple times a day, just prayed for God to heal the bones and make me whole again.

At the end of the week I headed back to the doctor in Butte, Montana. Money was pretty tight and I couldn't afford to sit out for a lengthy period of time so I was a bit nervous about what was going to come down. I just had faith that God was going to work a miracle. So six days after I broke it I go hobbling into the doctor's office on my crutches for new x-rays and a game plan.

The x-ray tech said, "Got a broken leg huh?" I responded, "Yeah, I had one." He asked what I meant and I said that God was going to heal my leg; he just looked at me like I was crazy. So we take my x-rays and I head off to the doctor's office to talk to him.

The doctor came in and he said, "I have good news and bad news, which one do you want to hear first?" I said, "I like good news, let's hear that first." He didn't know how to explain it, but my leg wasn't broken anymore. He was completely flabbergasted; there wasn't even a line on the new x-ray to indicate where a break had healed. The bone looked like it had never seen trauma before. I explained to him, with Brittney sitting next to me, that we'd prayed over it and I knew God was going to heal my leg.

Brittney just started crying. She wasn't new to being a Christian and praying, but she was pretty new to seeing God work like that.

The bad news was that I had about the worst sprain I could have in my ankle and it was going to be swollen, black and blue, and really sore for some time. I told him I could handle that, handed him my crutches, and walked out of his office.

We went to Walmart to get some anti-inflammatories he'd prescribed and they had one of those kid rides outside; the horse deal where you put a quarter in. So I climbed up on this horse and had Brittney take a picture of me spurring it just to show that I was back and hungry for more. I was back to competing within a week; I'd been healed.

"Out of It"

Before the 2008 season, I'd had an engagement fall apart just before my wedding. After that I wasn't even sure I wanted to compete in 2008. I was real upset and didn't know what I wanted to do; I was just confused about everything. I'd traveled to a couple rodeos but just didn't know what I wanted at that point in time.

Clint Cannon and I had talked about traveling together for a long time and I thought that given my mental state, it'd be good to travel with a close friend. People don't know the background on Clint and I, but at one point our families were almost going to live together. We were super close; Clint, Kirby, and Cody Cannon and I were basically raised as brothers. The day they were supposed to move to Colorado Clint's dad ended up getting a job in Texas so they stayed there.

We'd never really traveled together though. We were good friends and grew up together so we figured we could travel together. Clint hadn't made the NFR yet, but he was really close. He had been 16th the year before, which made him miss the Finals by one spot. Anyway, we started traveling together and his dad, Jay, came with us everywhere that year.

I figured it'd be the last year I'd rodeo. My heart just wasn't in it and given the previous year I just wasn't sure about much anymore. We started out at the Bucking Ball in Gillette, WY on New Years. I got a horse that nobody liked because he bucked everyone off, but I didn't really know much about him. He bucked hard and was hard to ride; I was 85 or 86 points and ended up winning 2nd. That was a good start to things, because it let me know I could still ride a rank one and it was still fun to prove that. It kind of lit a fire under me.

From there we went to the National Western in Denver and I rode well there in both rounds but didn't win any money. Next, we went to Odessa and I rode really well there and from Odessa we headed to Fort Worth. I've never had any luck in Fort Worth, ever. I ended up placing in both rounds and won the short round there.

At this point my confidence was growing so we headed on to San Antonio. My lowest score in San Antonio was around an 85. I ended up winning 2nd in all three rounds. I'd go back there and stand by the victory lap horse and as soon as I'd get on him, someone else would ride and kick me back down to 2nd. After three rounds of this the guy who holds the victory lap horse was apologizing for jinxing me. I told him I didn't come there to ride the horse around the arena; I'd come there to ride in the truck that the overall champion rode in. I could feel my want to win coming back. I wanted to go and ride.

From there we went to Jackson, Mississippi and I remember calling my dad and saying, "Dad, I've never been 90 before but I think I'm going to be 90 tonight. I can feel it." I was just in the zone, drawing well, riding good, and I was in shape. I was 89 the first night in Jackson and then drove back to San Antonio for the final round. I was 87 in the semifinals and headed to the finals.

I drew this horse, Wise Guy, for the final round and was winning it. I went over to that truck and the same guy was like, "Please don't get in the truck because then I'll feel like I've jinxed you again." I told him, "Nah, I'm going to get up in it." I ended up taking the victory lap in it and winning San Antonio. That was the biggest win thus far in my career and it had just fallen together so smoothly.

Things were just rolling; it was like a dream how smoothly things were going. Clint and I both made the short round in Austin, then we both made the short round in Tucson, and ended up back in Houston.

We were just getting the money like nobody else.

I ended up back in the semifinal round in Houston and it's 10 guys. I drew a horse called Good Time Charlie and Clint drew the horse Wise Guy that I'd won San Antonio on. Clint rides and was 88 or 89. I got on Good Time Charlie and was 97 points. I go to get off on the pickup man, and one second I was reaching around for him and the next second I remembered his horse walking on top of me! I was like, "Man, how did I get in this position?"

I got up, rubbed my head a little bit, and walked over to the fence. My brother met me at the fence and I remember saying, "Man, that horse was a little more than the first time I had him, I think he kicked me or something." We ended up watching it back on video and as I'd moved onto the pickup man, that horse had kicked me square in the head, that's how I'd fallen off and ended up underneath the pickup horse.

By the time we got from the arena back to the gate I was completely out of it. I didn't know where I was, that I'd just ridden a horse, nothing. I didn't know my own name! My brother was like, "Oh man…" because I'd won 2nd in the round, Clint had won the round, and we'd both made the final round.

I had a final eliminator horse, Magic Horse, which had set the arena record on at the NFR. I remember sitting in the locker room in a daze, watching people do their deal, and I was just loopy. I had no real idea what was going on around me. I made my way to the sports medicine room, I think my brother took me actually. He was on the phone with my dad trying to figure out what he should do with me. My dad said, "You give him two ibuprofen and some coffee, if we don't let him ride for $50,000 he's going to kill us all."

It comes time to ride. I've had coffee and probably more than two ibuprofen. Kirby and my brother are back there putting rosin on my rigging and glove. I was sitting off in this little room; I had ice all over my head and no shirt on. It was like trying to wake up from a deep sleep almost. They come back and said, "Okay man, we gotta go! The horses are loaded up!" Apparently I looked at them and said, "Go where?" They shouted, "Go where? It's the final round, it's $50,000, and you've got to ride!" I jumped up off the table and started off to the arena. They came running up behind me with my shirt and chaps because I was completely oblivious to the fact I didn't even have them on.

I just headed out there completely loopy. We get to where you go for right-handed or left-handed delivery and I go left. My brother just looks at me and says, "You just told me right-handed delivery, where are you going?" I just shrugged my shoulders and went back the other way; I was so out of it. I remember telling him to pull my rigging for me because he could pull it tighter than anybody else. I didn't know that I wasn't right, but everybody around me sure did. Inside I somehow knew I was going to need a little extra help on this one. I knew if I got hung up or something I was going to be zero help to anyone trying to help me.

Will Lowe rode, Kaycee Field rode, and then it was my turn. My brother gets down in the chute and helps me get my hand in my rigging and I'm just setting there. He was basically giving me a lesson like a kid about what I needed to do. I don't even remember any of this, just what people have told me in bits and pieces over time. My brother told them to go ahead and open the gate and this horse bucks, spooks, ducks, dives, he's all over. Throughout the ride the only thing I can remember is I stuck a foot up on his neck and in my brain I knew I needed to hustle and get it off or he was going to buck me off.

I remember right before I put my hand in I just prayed that the Lord would help me. I told Him I needed Him to be the pilot on this one. Even in the state I was in I knew I didn't need to be doing what I was doing. Next thing I knew I was 87.5 and winning Houston. I was "walking" back to the out gate and I'd made a bet with Dusty Tuckness that if I won Houston we'd go to Hawaii and I'd pay his way. Dusty said he thought I'd forgotten about it because of how jacked up I was. Apparently I remembered though because on the way back I made this hula dance move to him. He fist-pumped the air and just went, "Yes! He remembers!"

Clint came out, set the arena record, and won Houston; I finished second. I remember thinking it was an awesome ride and how happy I was to see my buddy doing so well. I vividly remember that ride. I went out there and met him halfway down the arena. I knew that he'd just cinched his way to the NFR by winning Houston. They put a picture in the paper and I remember we were both tearing up because we'd both made the Finals, and for me it had been a year where initially I questioned competing and for Clint he had come back from being so close to making it before.

I was still really out of it though. These reporters were trying to talk to me and I just kept telling them I didn't remember anything that had just happened. I really didn't; it was all foggy and hazy. I remember that before we left the house Clint and I had said that we were going to win first and second, it didn't matter who won what so long as we won.

There's a video somewhere of us talking to the reporters and you can tell how out of it I was. My eyes are just completely gazed over but my words were sincere. It was only March and we'd both made the NFR already; it was just a dream season. It took a while for my head to not be so sloshy. I'd drive places and not remember driving there or why I was there; it was scary.

That season I think there was only one weekend we went and didn't place and win money somewhere. We both went to the NFR in the top 5; Clint set a record for most regular season money won that year. It just all started rolling so early and it didn't seem to slow down. It was just a fun year and a dream season.

In rodeo you experience highs and lows. I've been on both ends of that. But that year when I left the house I just knew I was going to win. It was a dream season that culminated in me getting knocked out. That year set everything into motion for me to buy my place in Texas, get married, and lit the fire inside of me again. I wasn't even sure I wanted to compete anymore and three months later everything had changed, including my perspective.

Cody Kroul

Iowa cowboy Cody Kroul makes his home in Salmon, Idaho. Cody is an avid steer wrestler in the PRCA.

"Roanie"

My roan bulldogging horse has built himself quite a name in the rodeo world. He was born up on a mountain, weaned, and then they're kicked back out on the mountain until they're two years old.

I was up there outside Salmon, Idaho, night calving for a guy named Jud Whitworth. He'd bring me about four weanlings to the barn where I was night calving. We were down in the valley and had an indoor arena so every night I'd break the two year olds, four at a time.

So at night I'd go check on the herd every hour. If there was a cow getting ready to calve I'd run her into the barn for the night and then let them out the next day. I was up all night anyway; you don't get any sleep when you have to get up every hour. So I'd go work a horse then go check on the herd, come back and work another horse, and then go check on the herd.

Well, when these two year olds would get down into the valley they'd hardly seen a person much less anything else. They just come in loose in the trailer and as soon as they were out they'd all run to the back of the pen like a bunch of elk. They'd just stand there and snort.

The first day I'd run them into the round pen, rope them, and just try to get a halter on them. The second day I'd tried to ride all of them just to see if I could get the buck out of them. By the fourth day, I was out in the pasture tagging calves off this roan horse. He was just a quick learner and wasn't really scared of anything.

He just kept excelling faster and faster to the point that after about a month you could do just about any kind of ranch work on him. By the time he was three we were branding on him and he was just an all-around ranch horse. I almost sold him that year for $3,000 to an older rancher who wanted a laidback horse, but I just couldn't do it. So Jud just let me hold onto him awhile longer and kept working off of him.

Jud eventually gave him to me that year, we loaded all the others up and Jud just told me to take him as a thank you for all I'd done for him and all the horses I'd broke for him. He'd come to pick all the horses up and I was just telling him how athletic this horse was and what a quick learner he was. I was explaining they could probably get a fair bit of money for him. He loaded the other three and went to load Roanie last. Jud just handed the rope to me and said, "You've been doing such a good job with all the other ones, just keep this one as a gift." And that's how it all really started.

When he was four we decided to put him in a pick-up race in the local county fair. There were eight horses in the race and one of these horses was off the track, and he'd won the race three years in a row and was the obvious favorite. When the flag dropped all the other horses took off. Roanie was still pretty young and hadn't experienced anything like that before so he did a 360 spin almost and then took off. It was a 400-yard race and in those 400 yards he caught back up, passed six other horses, and missed winning to the favorite by a head.

After that we knew he could run, so for the next few years we just kept ranching on him and started roping off of him a little bit. We figured since he liked to race so much we'd try him in steer wrestling. I think I only ran by three or four steers and then we started jumping steers on him.

The first year I decided to compete with him I just went to local rodeos around the area, trying to fill my permit and get his confidence up. After that year, I decided to move away from ranching, did a little bit of big game hunting, and then these past two years I've started steer wrestling pretty aggressively.

2013 was probably the first year I took him and we went hard, from one rodeo right onto the next. We were 2nd in the go-round at Cheyenne, won a go-round in Pendleton, and won a round in the Waco finals. All in all, it was a really solid first year.

In 2013 I was the only one riding him, but in 2014 there were three of us riding him; my two traveling partners, Jacob Talley and Nick Guy, and myself. The three of us were riding him everywhere but about every rodeo I'd have one more guy ride him too. During the 4th of July Nick ended up being the highest money winner. He won $30,000 in five days with Roanie underneath him.

Casey Martin, Jacob, and myself rode him at Pendleton and I ended up fourth. Casey tied the arena record with a 3.8 and won Pendleton on him. Roanie was actually named "Horse of the Round-Up" for the year, which was pretty neat. Both of my horses, Keeper and Roanie, are headed to the NFR this year for guys to ride. Nick Guy will be competing on Roanie.

For a horse to come from a mountaintop in Idaho to heading to the Vegas lights in just a couple years, that's a superstar horse. I broke a lot of horses during those years I was night calving and looking back he always stands out. I think I'm lucky to have basically been the first person he ever came into contact with; he didn't have any bad habits developed.

He's just an all-around athlete. You can take him to a branding one week, hunting up the mountain the next, to a rodeo two days later, and he always excels. He just wanted a job; he needs to have a job. For him rodeo is fun, that's not his job. Branding, roping, hunting, packing elk, those are his jobs; that's work. He's not arena sour at all and he never has been. He knows a life outside of the arena.

He's seen and done it all and I think that's what makes him such an awesome athlete and he loves it. For him riding 20 miles in steep mountain country was work. Running three 4-7 second runs at a rodeo, getting fed better than ever, and hanging out is a cakewalk for him. He knows he's a rodeo horse now, but you can still take him and put anyone on him. He'll still go back and be a ranch horse or a laidback trail horse no problem.

He's given me a lot of avenues to go down because he's such an athlete and a superstar. He was born and bred to be a ranch horse; he wasn't necessarily bred to be the athlete he is. He could've been registered when I got him but I was going through so many horses that I just didn't even think about it at the time. That's why his name is just Roanie, he was a roan and so it was simple enough.

I just gave the ranch horse a chance to show himself and he's given me the opportunity to rodeo. He's drug thousands of calves to the fire when he was younger, and he's covered I don't know how many thousands of miles in some of toughest country Idaho has to offer. It's just kind of crazy now to look back on all the places I've taken him.

Some of the places he's been people wouldn't take their $500 horse and I have probably a $100,000 horse. I have the upmost confidence in him, no matter the job at hand. I think that's what made him so tough and what keeps him going, he's not even 11 years old and he just keeps excelling every year.

Editor's Note: Roanie would go on to help Nick Guy win Round 1 at the 2014 Wrangler National Finals Rodeo and place in 4 additional rounds.

Trent Willmon

Trent Willmon is a prominent singer/songwriter hailing from Afton, Texas. As a songwriter Trent has written songs for Brad Paisley, Eric Church, and Little Big Town. He's know for penning Steel Magnolia's #1 hit "Keep On Lovin' You" as well as Montgomery Gentry's "Back When I Knew It All".

Trent has also had a successful solo career, releasing 2 albums (2004's "Trent Willmon" and 2006's "A Little More Livin') on Columbia Records and a 3rd independent record, "Broken In" in 2008 on Compadre. Trent went on to make his acting debut in 2008 in "Palo Pinto Gold" alongside Roy Clark and Mel Tillis.

Trent splits his time between Afton, TX and Nashville, TN. When he's not busy working Trent values the time he has with his daughter and his girlfriend. Given the opportunity, he's always eager to rope, ride, and work cows.

"Although I knew how to swing a rope some and worked with horses some growing up, I didn't start team roping until my early 20's. I knew it was never going to be an option for me to choose that as a career. There is a big difference in the dedication and mentality of someone who is a career roper and someone who enjoys it as a hobby. I am definitely the latter."

"Rustlers"

Years ago when I first moved to Tennessee to be a rich and famous household name (still working on that), I was living in a little cabin heated by a little wood burning cook stove and no running water. I was working for a fellow named Randy Huston who had a couple hundred head of mama cows. He was a rancher from New Mexico who had also been a songwriter, publisher, and cowboy poet. We still worked cattle the old way, roping and dragging and branding, and I loved it.

In addition to farm and ranch work I was also writing songs and setting up meetings with publishers to try to land a songwriting deal. I also had become close friends with a few budding songwriters who were also country folk and/or ranch and farm kids. We were dirt poor but happy as can be chasing our dreams. Times would get lean occasionally and we would live on venison and the occasional six pack of cheap beer.

At one such time, one of my said good friends had mentioned

how nice it would be to have beef instead of whitetail. No one would miss a calf all that much and it would help out through the winter.

I insisted that Mr. Huston was quite observant and that he would indeed miss a calf. End of discussion.

I had to go into town that day to play my songs for a publisher. As I was driving back, my girlfriend called and said I needed to stop by her house and she would explain why when I got there. When I arrived she informed me that 3 of my friends had indeed poached a beef and had taken it to my cabin in the woods to butcher it, because it was in the middle of nowhere and no one would know of the crime. I was beyond furious!

As I sped down the one lane road, I was thinking of how I would certainly lose my job, if not wind up in jail. I'd seen Mr. Huston lose his cool a time or two. I rounded the curve to my house and there it was, carcass hanging from the tree in my front yard. Idiots didn't even have sense enough to at least hang it in the backyard! The hide was draped across the fence in broad daylight; Lazy Y Bar brand still intact. The skull had a .45 long colt bullet hole between the eyes. I grew angrier and angrier by the second.

The guilty party was on the porch celebrating. My three amigos were there drinking cold beer as if they hadn't just committed a hang-able offense. I chewed their asses, threw the hide in the bushes, and demanded that they put the damn carcass elsewhere. They all laughed and said that if Randy Huston happened to stop by they would say it was a deer. "What?? An elk, maybe! It's 300lbs!"

They all laughed and ignored me, opening more beers and slapping me on the back. "If he says anything, we will just say it broke its leg and we had to put it down."

"Randy was a veterinarian!" I was out of my mind by this point. "He will obviously know that isn't true!" I cussed them all. Here I was an accomplice to a crime with my three best friends. I was going to lose my job, and it was going to be a long, cold winter...

After a couple hours of torturing me, the fellas finally broke the truth: the heifer had indeed broken its leg by accident, and they had asked Randy if they could butcher her. He agreed, and in true cowboy fashion they all saw a great opportunity to fill a freezer as well as play a great prank on their good buddy Trent. I must say, I did finally laugh about it, but it took me a couple days to cool down. I guess in a way, that's how you know your part of the cowboy family... if they #%*! with you.

Clint Cooper

Clint Cooper makes his home in Decatur, Texas with his wife Amber and their two sons, Casen and Canden. Clint is the oldest son of 8x World Champion Roy Cooper, as well as the oldest brother to Clif and Tuf Cooper.

Clint has qualified for the National Finals five times, won Calgary Stampede and
Cheyenne Frontier Days in the same year, and is co-owner of "Sweetness", 3x PRCA Horse of the Year.

Clint has countless wins to his name, including being the co-champion at Rancho Mission Viejo Rodeo in San Juan Capistrano, CA as well as winning the National Western Stock Show & Rodeo in Denver, CO. In 2011 Clint won Round 7 of the NFR with a time of 7.6 and placed in four other rounds. At the 2014 NFR Clint placed in 4 rounds.

When Clint's at home he spends his time practicing with his brothers and brother-in-law Trevor Brazile. He enjoys basketball, hunting, fishing, and watching his son's football team.

"Greatest Accomplishment"

In rodeo people often ask what you feel is your greatest accomplishment, whether that's qualifying for the NFR or winning certain rodeos. I joined the PRCA in 2002 and it was pretty rocky for a couple years. I just couldn't seem to get things rolling and I knew I was capable of doing better and being better.

In 2004 things seemed to finally start clicking. I kicked off the year by winning the National Western in Denver, which helped boost my confidence and then things seemed to die down again. Come July I knew I needed to start putting things together if I wanted a guaranteed spot at the NFR, which would have been my first NFR appearance.

I headed up to Calgary Stampede for the first time ever, and I didn't really know what to expect. Well I ended up winning it, which was not what I had expected or planned at all. From Calgary we headed down to Cheyenne for Frontier Days. CFD is just a giant lottery with big calves; it's tough and it's famous for being that way. Cheyenne is a bit more "cowboy" centered than some and that's reflected in the competition and the stock.

So roughly two weeks after I won Calgary I ended up turning around and winning Cheyenne Frontier Days. I'd won two of the biggest rodeos back-to-back. Winning Calgary was unexpected, winning Calgary and Cheyenne was almost unbelievable. That, in combination with that fact that I was guaranteed heading to the NFR, was almost too much to comprehend at once. I was 22 and just felt on top of the world. I felt like I'd finally established myself as an individual.

My first time to the NFR I went in 6th and it went fairly well. I won Round 7 and placed in four other rounds. I ended up 8th overall that year, but whenever anyone asks what my greatest career accomplishment is, it's winning Calgary and Cheyenne back-to-back that year.

"Brothers"

Probably one of the most memorable things for me will always be the year my brothers (Clif and Tuf) and I all qualified for the National Finals in the same year. It was just such a blessing for us to all make it in the same event, the same year, and it was our first time for all three of us to be there at once. Just to experience that together made the whole deal that much sweeter.

I mean we've grown up together, looked up to our dad our whole lives, practiced together, competed against each other, and to have all those years, hours of practice, and countless rodeos come together like that just was an awesome feeling.

Not only were we all at the National Finals together, but also you get to help each other and support each other. I mean if I'm not winning then I want them to be. Yeah it's a competition, but that's my family and we want the best for each other. Just to be able to back into the box at the NFR and have my brothers helping me and then to turn around and be able to do the same for them, it's an amazing feeling.

We'd talk to each other about the calves the night before and break things down; you have your own team when you have your family.

We all won a round that year. Tuf actually won the 10th Round and I tied for second in that. To have us all compete at the top of our game, have our family there, have our dad in the stands, it was truly a life-changing experience.

It's tough to compete against your family, but I'd just as soon compete against my brothers as anyone else.

Sterling Furr

Bull rider Sterling Furr is from Boerne, TX and currently attends Southwest Texas Junior College where he studies Wildlife Management.

Sterling started riding bulls when he was 14, traveling to various youth rodeos across Texas. When he was 16 Sterling decided to enter the Tejas Rodeo in Bulverde, TX, an open rodeo that would allow him to compete on another level. From there he started working his way up the ranks. He's competed in the Junior PBR and at the PBR Finals three years (2008, 2009, 2010).

As soon as he turned 18 Sterling bought his permits and started competing in both PBR and PRCA events.

Beyond the rodeo arena, Sterling's favorite hobbies are hunting and fishing.

"Experience"

In 2012, I went to my first PRCA Extreme Bull event. Needless to say I was pretty nervous, since I'd never experienced something on that level before. I entered in the event in Fort Worth, TX and my dad came along for the ride since I was a fresh 18. It was a two-night event, Tuesday and Wednesday, and I was scheduled to ride on Wednesday.

We got there a little bit early. I walked back to the locker room and quickly realized it was filled with my idols and my heroes. J.W. Harris, Steve Woolsey, Parker Breding, and a few others were all mingling around. I wasn't used to being in a locker room having just competed at open rodeos and a few PRCA rodeos. I tossed my gear bag down and just tried to take it all in.

It was pretty cool being in a locker room; it's got a different atmosphere to it. I got to hang my rope next to J.W. Harris and talk to him a little bit, he was a really cool guy and real nice to me.

It's getting closer to go time at this point, so I'm getting all my stuff together and found out I've drawn this bull that was owned by Diamond S Bucking Bulls. He was a good-looking red bull; I asked around and found out what I needed to know about him. I ended up getting a re-ride; he came out and hung his horn on the chute.   I got a re-ride bull from Wildcard Rodeos called Smokey White Devil. The night before

Chandler Bownds was 88 on him in the short round, so I figured if I rode him in the long round I was going to get a decent score. I rode him and was 84.5 on him. He hadn't had as good of a trip as he had the night before. I still made the short round though and I was so stoked. I was ready.

I headed back to the locker room to catch my breath. This was my second bull with a third to go. They run the show pretty fast so I'm running back and forth getting stuff ready. I was only familiar with one bull out of the 10 bucking in the short-round, I knew the 2012 bucking bull of the year, Cat Ballou.

I'm back in the locker room and re-taping, talking, getting focused for the short round, and as I'm getting ready my dad comes back. I looked at him and he said, "Son, I've just got to say one thing, you'd better have your riding jeans on." I thought to myself for a moment and at that point I knew exactly what bull I had drawn, Cat Ballou.

Chills ran up and down my spine, my first Extreme Bull events, my first time making the short round, and I'd drawn the bucking bull of the year. I was really excited but kind of freaking out at the same time.

It's time for the short round and they run this bull in the chutes. He weighs every bit of 2,000 pounds, real pretty brown and white bull, just big and solid muscle. Just the way he looked was intimidating to a degree, you knew when he bucked there was going to be a lot of force behind it.

I looked over at my travel buddy and asked him if he was nervous for me, he just looked back at me and went, "Oh yeah, I'm nervous for you." That didn't really help my nerves at the moment and I thought it best to not ask any more questions.

I lowered myself down onto his broad back, got everything just right, and nodded my head. It took about three jumps but he bucked me off. I hit the ground, I just got up, and thought, "Well, that was pretty crazy." Didn't see much point in pitching a fit or beating myself up about it.

As I was walking back to the chutes I heard Don Gay announce, "Man, for this to be your first Extreme Bulls event, make the short round, and draw that bull, that's a pretty tough break." That's just the way it goes though, sometimes you draw the ones you want, sometimes you draw the ones you need, and sometimes you draw out of your league. I just drew out of my league that night.

I went back to the locker room and while I was putting my stuff up some of the guys back there struck up a conversation with me; they acknowledged it was a tough break to draw how I did. Despite everything I felt good about myself to have gone to my first event and made the first impression that I had made. I do believe in second chances, but I really look at first impressions, especially professionally and riding bulls. It doesn't matter who I'm in front of, I just really try to make a good first impression because I think people remember you by that.

I ended up getting a taste of what the Extreme Bulls was like right off the bat; real quick lesson to learn. After the event, we were on the way home and I was already thinking about what the next one was going to be like.

The following Extreme Bulls event I competed at I was far less nervous. I knew what to expect. I kept replaying what had happened in Fort Worth, I needed to improve on that performance. I was headed back to the locker room and on the way Don Gay pulled me aside. He said, "Son, I was really impressed with your performance at the last Extreme Bulls. Tonight you're in a new town, you've got a bull that's really mean, but they don't make a bull that'll give you a nicer ride." I was thinking, "Oh, first I get Cat Ballou and now I get this…."The bull was out of Frontier Rodeo and I ended up riding him really nicely and things starting clicking together.

Everything that happened at Fort Worth just seemed to set the bar. I can't say I'd look forward to a rematch with Cat Ballou, but given the opportunity I'd give it all I had. He bucked and bucked hard, but I feel like I know what to expect now. I feel like it'd be my turn to get back at him and make things even.

Sarah Thompson

Sarah Thompson was born and raised in Bundella, New South Wales, Australia. Sarah grew up on her family's cattle and farming station. After she finished school she spent two years performing in a traveling horse circus touring Australia and New Zealand.

In 2010 Sarah came to the United States for the World Equestrian Games and met the Riata Ranch Cowboy Girls, a trick roping and trick riding performance team based in California. Sarah just completed her fourth season in a row on the team, traveling all over the country performing at various rodeos.

In 2014 Sarah was crowned the Royal Australian Trick Riding Champion at the Sydney Royal Easter Show.

Though she grew up without any rodeo experience or exposure, Sarah has quickly become addicted to the sport, both the opportunities it presents and the lifestyle it allows her to lead.

Sarah spends her time traveling between Australia, Canada, and the United States performing on the rodeo circuit, at special events, as well as training and working on various ranches and stations.

"Opportunities"

For me, having been given the opportunity to tell a story, I think the best story I can tell is about having a good attitude, trust, confidence and acceptance in the opportunities that life offers you. How if you are willing to be patient and driven with what you want from this life, that it will lead you along pathways you didn't even know you were meant to take. To find something that you didn't even know you were looking for... For me, that was rodeo.

Growing up in Australia on our family station combined with support from my family, and my determination, passion, desire, and stubbornness, I felt a push to go outside the "norm" of working with horses, to realize I wanted something more.

When I was 17, I watched Dan James, a partner in Double Dan Horsemanship, present a roman riding, liberty and horsemanship demonstration. That just blew my mind! Right at that moment I knew that this style of riding was something I needed to know more about.

That afternoon (after some liquid courage), I approached this man they called Dan and introduced myself, nervous as all hell, but knowing it was what I needed to do. We shook hands (I still have no idea what I said because of the nerves) but at the end of the conversation I had his card in my hand and was told to contact him. I immediately went home and did just that.

For two years after that, I worked with Dan learning and absorbing what I could about liberty training and horses. Every day I looked at a picture on his fridge of a beautiful blonde-headed trick rider on a palomino horse, Niki Cammaert, Professional Trick Rider (now known as Niki Flundra). Dan also had this book on his shelf about a group of talented ladies, they called themselves the Riata Ranch Cowboy Girls and they were a professional trick riding and trick roping team.

To me what these ladies did was so astonishing and classy. Rodeo, performing, cowboy hats, spandex, traveling all across America and Canada…what did I know about that? I knew that that's what I wanted to be a part of, but how? These ladies seemed invincible. How could I possibly be a part of something untouchable and unique?

In 2010, Dan was asked to perform in the opening of the World Equestrian Games in Lexington Kentucky with a liberty and roman-riding act and he had hired me to help him out. I packed my bags from the circus in Australia and took my first trip across the big pond to America. Little did I know the opportunities that were once again going to be available to me if I just took the chance.

Within an hour of being at the grounds, a car pulled up curbside; Dan was in the driver's seat with a car full of women. I just thought, "Of course he has a car full of women…" and climbed into the backseat. Dan turned to me and said, "Sarah meet the Riata Ranch Cowboy Girls, they are performing with us here." I was slightly speechless as each of them individually shook my hand and introduced themselves.

Dan spoke about the liberty horses he had there and the appreciation he had for the lady that owned them and the process it took to get them from Canada to Kentucky. Naturally I asked Dan who this lady was, "You remember the picture on my fridge at home of the trick rider? Niki? Well she is starting a liberty act and these are her horses".

I couldn't believe it, for the next week I hung out with the Riata Ranch Cowboy Girls and worked with Niki's liberty team; I was just tickled. To me this was the greatest privilege, to be among so many wonderful entertainers and people I admired.

After the WEG came to an end and we were getting ready to leave, Jennifer Nicholson, Executive Director of Riata Ranch, handed me her business card. She said, "Sarah, if you're ever in California and you want to come and train at the ranch with us, call me."

Prior to this point I was ready to fly back home and continue my life in the circus, living in a 9' x 4' bunkhouse room on wheels. Upon my return to Australia a fellow carney informed me there would be no more touring that year, the circus was done for the season and I had free time to do what I pleased.

Instantly I emailed Jennifer. It seemed like in just days I was on a plane to San Francisco to walk horseback down Pier 39 with the Riata Girls, Cotton Rosser and the Flying U Rodeo Company. They were promoting The Grand National Rodeo at The Cow Palace, announced by Bob Tallman. Looking back, and knowing what I know about rodeo now, I realize that wasn't such a bad way to be introduced to the sport.

I spent three weeks in California with the girls training in trick riding and learning what their program is about. They taught me so much about their business in rodeo and what it takes to survive in the industry. The girls and the ranch opened my mind to how Riata wasn't just a trick riding and roping team it is more than that. It was all a perfect fit and I was hooked. Rodeo, fast horses, a fantastic group of girls, traveling, performing, showmanship, and trick riding.

Over the past four years I have worked hard on my trick riding and showmanship to be on the performance team and just to be able to perform with the girls in countless PRCA rodeos across the country.

During the fall of 2011 after my first summer with Riata, I decided I wanted to go and explore and live in southern Alberta, Canada with some great friends of mine who were living on a ranch up there. As I arrived I was told that the following day we were to muster (gather) cattle for a local bronc rider and his wife, a lady who "did some trick riding" on the neighboring ranch.

We drove towards the Rocky Mountains in our tiny, banged up, two door Chevrolet with one red door, the hood ratchet strapped down, duct tape in every corner, and more rust than paint, to the 'Shodaree

Ranch'. We headed to the barn to saddle horses and begin our day and sure enough, as I walked down the barn aisle Niki Cammaert Flundra comes walking the other way. "Hi Sarah I'm Niki, I've been looking forward to meeting you for quite some time". She gave me a massive hug while I tried to form words.

I couldn't believe it, out of all the places in Canada for my life to lead me it was to live across the river from my inspiration. Here I was standing before the woman I'd idolized as the photo on the fridge, the brazen, blonde-haired trick rider.

To top it all off that day, Niki even let me ride the infamous palomino horse from the photo, Rebel. I'd watched countless YouTube videos of Niki and Rebel for years, now I was helping her gather cows and riding Rebel. Talk about a rush!

Since then, Niki has generously offered to share with me her knowledge of liberty training and hires me when Riata has their off-season to help her with her horses for her own professional act.

With courage and confidence in what my life has offered to me, I've been able to take the opportunities that were in front of me and grow from them. Sometimes I moved places where I didn't know a person, or have traveled to unfamiliar places without knowing what was going to even happen or how. I ended up having Riata and Niki, the two most influential people in my life, and the impact they've given my life has been immeasurable.

They've given me direction, and they've given me rodeo.

Billy Bob Brown

Billy Bob Brown is from Eastland, Texas. It's been a long running joke in his family that Bob was born with a rope in his hand; both his parents were active in the rodeo circuit and his mother was even a WPRCA

With the guidance of his dad and late grandfather, Billy Bob Brown began his roping career. In 2009 he was crowned the Texas High School Rodeo Association State Champion Calf Roper, the next year he became the THSRCA State Champion Team Roper. In 2013 he was the College National Champion in Team Roping and won the All Around. In 2014 he was named the Resistol Rookie of The Year in the All Around.

Billy Bob Brown attends Tarleton State University in Stephenville, Texas and is an active participant on their rodeo team as well. He's majoring in Business with a minor in Agriculture, fulfilling a promise he made to his parents that he'd get a college education while competing. He's set to graduate in May 2015.

"Miracle Baby"

When I was born I wasn't supposed to live, everything pointed to the fact I wasn't supposed to be here.

I was born September 2, 1991 with a collapsed lung and my heart was in the wrong cavity, neither of which is a good deal, much less for a newborn. The doctors at Hendricks Medical Center came into my mom's room and told my parents that they were going to have to do surgery to try and save me. It was a type of invasive surgery they'd never done before, no doctor on staff had ever seen a baby born with these defects before, but they were going to do their best to save me.

I was hooked up to tons of machines; looking back at pictures of it it's not a pretty sight. Here I was this tiny baby with tubes, needles, and machines all around me trying to help me survive this high-risk surgery. Miraculously I made in through the surgery but I was far from safe. The doctors didn't know if I'd live an hour or live a year.

I was so sick that I didn't even have a name for the first week of my life because the doctors realistically didn't think I would live. One day the doctors came in and told my mom she could name me, I was getting stronger and they felt that I was safe to go home. I was out of immediate danger, though they had no idea what life had in store for me.

When I went home the hospital made a video for my family dubbing me "The Miracle Baby of 1991", we still have the video at the house. It featured all the babies born, but they had a special segment on my journey and my fight to live.

You know the scene in the "Lion King" where he holds the baby cub up in his hand? When they were videoing my dad took me out into the middle of the cow pasture and kind of did the same thing, that's how they chose to end the video. It was a miracle I was even there.

I don't really remember any of it, but it has affected me in certain ways. I'm not exactly the biggest person in the world. When I played basketball in high school I could only play a certain number of minutes and then I'd have to sit out for a few. I'd often come from roping practice to play in a basketball game and it just took me a little bit longer to get my air back. It takes me longer to get in shape than most people. I feel like I have to work twice as hard in the gym as anyone else, not that I'm complaining because it's helped me develop an incredible work ethic.

When it comes to rodeo I just have to work harder at some things than most people, but life on the road and the crazy schedule doesn't seem to affect me too much. My body just doesn't work like most people's does, and that's what people don't see. People can see my success, I've been very blessed in my career thus far. They don't see the struggle and work ethic behind it all. It's made me so driven, I think because I know it could have been so much worse. I just have to wake up everyday and chase my dreams because I was kept here on Earth to do that.

It's a blessing I'm here, the doctors and the Lord kept me here. I'm grateful that I have the opportunity to tell kids they do have a chance, no matter what they're told. Everything leading up to this has given me a sense of direction. In addition to rodeo, I want to help kids and people in general know that they have a chance. There are people who get beat down and they're told they don't have a chance in hell, you know, they need to think again though. Everyone has a chance; it's just your decision and it's up to you to make it happen.

Carter Williams

Carter grew up on various working ranches learning how to work cows and handle horses from a young age. Carter has been a pickup man at rodeos for the past 16 years and doesn't plan on retiring anytime soon.

When he's not picking up, Carter spends his free time team roping and just being a cowboy. Carter tends to his own herd, raises horses, and breaks colts. Carter Williams is from Wilcox, Arizona.

"Cowpunchers"

I was straight out of college and had just moved to Wilcox. There were these two older men that lived down in Wilcox who were real cowpunchers. They were well into their 70's and my young and eager work ethic just happened to catch their eye. They asked me to go and help them one time and I happily obliged.

I jumped in and off we went. I was the youngest guy and all three of us were crammed in a single cab pick-up. One old man was named Jack and he was maybe 5'3", a really little guy. He always reminded me of the cartoon character Yosemite Sam. He was driving so the seat is damn up near the dashboard. I stand near 6'2" so it wasn't the most comfortable thing in the world. The other guy who was with us was named Chad, and I remember he'd always roll his own cigarettes. Chad wasn't much of a cowboy, but he loved to roll his own cigarettes, drink whiskey, and talk.

We left about 4am to head to this ranch; it was still dark outside when we left. Jack takes off and we're probably going 90mph down this dirt road and we come up on this dip in the road. It's the kind of sharp dip that kind of makes you feel like you're riding a rollercoaster and you've left your stomach back on the side of the road. Well Jack is just driving like he's running from the law and Chad is on the other side of me trying to roll a cigarette in the dark.

That truck hit that dip in the road and it kind of jostled all of us about. Miraculously Chad never dropped his cigarette. Pretty quickly Chad coughed, I think it'd startled him quite a bit, and he coughed up one of his teeth! He spit the tooth out in his hand and I just looked at him and asked, "Chad, what are you going to do with that tooth?" Chad was a married man, his wife's name was Irene. He turned to me with a sparkle in his eye and said, "Oh, I'm making Irene a necklace. Every tooth I lose I just slip it into my front pocket and then I add it to the rest when I get back home."

We chuckled a good bit over that one; it was clearly visible that Irene's necklace probably had a good half dozen teeth on it already. But I guess you really didn't need teeth to smoke cigarettes and drink whiskey. That was one of my first real experiences going out with the older guys and I actually became pretty good friends with then. We ended up working together a lot.

"For Sale By Owner, See Room 322"

Once I was working for a rodeo company down in Spearville, Arizona during the 4th of July. We'd just come back from the arena that morning. We'd been out there feeding all the stock prior to performance time. This guy Bobby owned all the bucking bulls in the company and another guy Scott owned all the broncs. Well, Bobby had just bought himself a brand new Ford 550 Powerstroke with a big flatbed on it. That truck probably didn't even have a 1,000 miles on it at this point. He'd parked it at the hotel and it was sort of facing out towards the street.

Scott and I were talking about his new truck and we realized the way it was parked it kind of looked like it was for sale; angled up towards the road and looking brand new from the dealership. We went into the lobby and found a piece of cardboard and a marker and wrote "For Sale, $1500 or best offer" and put Bob's phone number and room number on the sign. We chuckled to ourselves and headed back to our rooms.

That evening we show up to the rodeo grounds and Bob pulls in and he's pretty ticked off. Scott and I just chuckled and egged him on a bit, "Bob, what's wrong?"

"Goddangit, I couldn't get a nap today. I had people knocking on my door and calling my phone all afternoon. Shoot, some asshole put my truck up for sale! This one guy knocked on my door three or four times trying to buy it for $1500!"

He was so mad and was grumpy all night. Finally Scott and I broke it to him that we'd been the ones who had put his truck up for sale and man, he was steaming for a few days! Today we luckily can look back and laugh about that brand new truck for sale for $1500 and people disturbing Bob's naptime.

Tim O' Connell

Tim O'Connell hails from Zwingle, Iowa, but calls Marshall, Missouri home.

In 2010 Tim won the Wisconsin High School State bull riding, however, following a bad bull riding wreck at the National High School Finals Rodeo, he switched to riding bareback horses.

The 22-year-old cowboy has since taken the bareback world by storm; in 2013 he was named the PRCA Resistol Rookie of The Year. In 2013 and 2014 Tim won the average and year-end title at the Great Lakes Circuit Champion in bareback.

Tim headed to the 2014 Wrangler National Finals Rodeo sitting 4th in the world and would go on to win Round 4 in the bareback.

"Do You Remember This Road Ever Being Red?"

One time I was traveling with Kaycee Fields, Jessy Davis, and Kaycee's roommate. We were driving from Casper, WY, to Colorado Springs, CO, on to Sheridan, WY, and then back for the short round in Casper, WY.

So after we went from the long round at Casper to Colorado Springs, we headed on to Sheridan. Jessy jumped out in Sheridan and headed up to Canada to the Calgary Stampede. Kaycee was headed there after the short round in Casper so in the meantime his wife and their 1-year-old baby hopped in the van with us.

After we dropped Jesse off we went to this guy's house in Wyoming. Ironically the guy used to pickup with my dad back in the 80's. We spent most of the night swapping stories about that. The next morning we got up and left out of there in the early afternoon. We were going to make it to Casper in plenty of time and didn't see a reason to rush.

Along the way, we stopped at a convenience store in the middle of nowhere. Well, when we pulled out of the parking lot Kaycee, unbeknownst to us, took a wrong turn and headed back towards Gillette on I-90….which was in the complete opposite direction.

We'd been driving a solid two hours when all of a sudden the road went from a smooth pavement to this reddish-color. Almost at the exact same time Kaycee and I looked at each other and went, "Do you remember the road ever being this reddish color?"

I'd been on the phone with my uncle earlier and he thought we were going in the wrong direction, however I felt sure Kaycee knew where he was going. I mean he's a 2x World Champion, so I felt sure he knew how to get from Sheridan to Casper and I wasn't about to say anything.

Well, once we figured out that we were indeed going in the wrong direction, Kaycee went to recalculate arrival times on his phone's GPS. We went from arriving in Casper three hours early to being there two hours after the rodeo was supposed to start.

We figured that out and that's when Kaycee figured out just how fast that van could go! I had never been in a van with a wife and a baby and here we are taking these back roads trying to make up for lost time; Kaycee is taking gravel roads and we're just rolling at about 90mph. We're taking 45-degree turns at 50 or 60mph. It was like the rodeo version of "Fast and Furious" out there on these Wyoming back roads.

I don't know how he did it and I probably don't really want to, but we managed to pull into Casper an hour before the rodeo started. Things went from us not being sure we'd even make the short round to the fact that we had plenty of time to get ready.

Kaycee's wife was surprisingly cool about everything too. I thought she'd be freaking out with the baby but she was great. We were straight cruising those back roads trying to make up time and she just went along with it.

Kaycee ended up winning Casper and I finished 4th or 5th, I was pretty happy with the outcome, needless to say. Considering we weren't sure we would ever make the rodeo I couldn't complain about things too much.

Jim Watkins

Jim Watkins was born in Fairfax, Missouri.

Jim got his start in the Little Britches Rodeo and competed through his high school years. Throughout high school he competed in bareback, bull riding, steer wrestling, and tie-down roping. He qualified for the High School Finals in bareback and tie-down roping, adding bull riding to that list in his senior year.

After high school, he went on to graduate from Sul Ross State University. During college Jim would compete in PRCA events and then after college he turned pro full time. Jim competed at rodeos all over the country from Cheyenne to Cow Palace. He also judged at various rodeos including Cheyenne Frontier Days, Odessa, Deadwood, Pecos, Pikes Peak or Bust, and others for several years.

Jim also made bull ropes for men such as Harry Thompkins, Wacey Cathey, Bobby Steiner, and Adam and Gilbert Carrillo. Jim made Jim Sharp's ropes throughout his entire career. He stopped making ropes in 1993.

He was the coach for Odessa College's rodeo team from 1984-1998, coaching the likes of Jim Sharp, Ty Murray, Jerome Davis, Cimmaron Gerke, Ryan Gray, Adam and Gilbert Carrillo, and D.J. Domangue. All in all, Jim Watkins coached 11 National Event Champions and the 1989 NIRA National Championship Team.

Jim was honored as Coach of the Year for the NIRA in 2009 and retired just a few months later. He was inducted into the Texas Rodeo Cowboy Hall of Fame in 2010.

Today, Jim continues to act as a coach and a mentor to many of his students. He spends his time being an active voice for the sport of rodeo, being a devoted husband to his wife of over 50 years, a fantastic father to his three grown children who each all won a Texas State High School Championship, and a grandfather to his four grandchildren.

"Coach"

There are lots of things you tell cowboys during difficult times. I've been fortunate to have guys come through my program at Odessa and they stay in touch with me. Sometimes they'll call me up during the NFR or another major rodeo and sometimes they'll just call to visit. That's always good; I like having that relationship with kids I've taught.

Cimmaron Gerke was definitely a special student of mine. I remember once he had a rodeo the coming weekend and on his way there, probably a few days early, his stomach started giving him terrible pains. He stopped in a town on the way and went to the hospital where they told him he had appendicitis and needed to have emergency surgery. So they did the appendectomy right then and there. Four days later, Cimmaron rode at the Regional Finals in New Mexico so he could make it to the College Finals that year. He was tough enough then, and still is, that four days after surgery he came and got on his Regional Finals Horse so he could make it College Finals. He actually ended winning the Regional Finals and College Finals that year. Most cowboys wouldn't have been able to do that, but the ones that are special have that drive in them.

I first noticed Jim Sharp in junior rodeos; he and my son Todd competed together. I think when my kids all won their respective Texas State High School Championships that helped my program grow. When Jim Sharp came here and I started coaching him it seemed that every bull rider in the country wanted to come to Odessa. I got to know Cody Lambert pretty well; I'd helped him put on a bull riding school at Sul Ross. Just networking and connecting like that helped the program keep growing. We were getting bigger and bigger and the level of athletes was improving. Shawn McMullan came to me as a college freshman. His first year he didn't win the championship, but he went on to be a two-time National Intercollegiate Tie-Down Champion. He won the College National Title in 1989 and 1990. Ty Murray won three National Titles for me; the bull riding, bronc riding, and the all-around. Those guys helped build my program. They helped draw kids to the school and to the program. It just snowballed from there.

In 1992 I had Jerome Davis, Adam Carrillo, and Gilbert Carrillo all in the same year, three great bull riders on one team. I had the honor of inducting the Carrillos at the PBR Ring of Honor Ceremony at the 2014 PBR World Finals. One of the things I said in my speech was there wasn't just Adam and there wasn't just Gilbert, even when they talked about each other they split everything they did. They were just a package deal and everyone was trying to recruit them. Every school knew that you couldn't separate them, since they're identical twins. Luckily I got them and Jerome Davis at the same time.

When it came time for Odessa to host our college rodeo that year, we put it on in the coliseum and it was up to the team to raise the sponsorship money and get the buckles donated. Adam and Gilbert got their parents to donate the buckle for bull riding because they swore one of them was bound win it; they were positive thinkers so to them that's just how it was going to be. Sure enough their parents donated the buckles and then Jerome Davis won it. Adam and Gilbert came out onto the arena floor and donated this buckle they were sure they were going to win to their teammate. There was no malice or competitiveness. They were genuinely excited that Jerome had won the bull riding.

Adam and Gilbert always told me if one of them got hurt they'd never have to turn out their bulls. They joked they would just go change shirts in the car and the same guy could get on both bulls. Thank goodness we never had to do that, as far as I know we never had to do that. If they ever did it, I sure never found out about it!

My wife once told me that I'd never grown up, because I got new kids to play with every year the whole time I was coaching. It's been so good and they call me all the time. D.J. Domangue invited me to his wedding; he sends me pictures of him fishing. D.J. came here from Louisiana, didn't make it too long, left, and then wanted to come back. I decided to give him a second chance and let him come back so long as he was dedicated to making his grades. We didn't have bulls at that time so we would go to Steve Power's arena in Midland, TX. Our athletic department had trainers for us and a trainer would go with us to practice every day. When we went to ride bulls they'd just hop in the van and come with us. The year D.J. came back our trainer was a girl, Tammy Williams. She was in the nursing program, but she was a fantastic trainer.

One day when we got through riding bulls, we dropped Tammy off at the sports center, and we were headed back to my place. The guys could get their trucks and we could start practicing the timed events under the lights. Anyway, right after we dropped Tammy off D.J. made the announcement, "One day I'm going to marry that girl." He'd never dated her or anything at all; he just stated that he was going to marry her.

About four years later, I got a phone call, "Coach, this is D.J. I want to know if you want to come to my wedding." He'd been competing, been to the NFR, everything, so I asked him who he was going marry. "Who'd I say I was going to marry?" I almost dropped the phone, "You can't be serious…" Sure enough, he married Tammy and now they have a beautiful family together.

Ryan Gray is another great cowboy who came through the program. He and his family have been really good to me. They often provide us with tickets to the NFR and he checks in on my wife and I. He's just a good person.

I've been so fortunate to coach some special guys. I'd always research and go scout when they were in high school. I'd have an idea of who I wanted, but there was always a process to picking kids I thought had the potential. Ty Murray was a sophomore in high school when he first started catching my attention. My wife was actually watching his National High School Rodeo scores. She told me, "You'd better keep your eye on this kid! He goes everywhere and wins everything!" I didn't do much about it until he was a junior in high school. Everybody wanted Ty Murray, but fortunately he chose to come to Odessa.

I recruited a kid from California once, David Howard. He was a talented bronc rider so I went down and invited him and his folks out to lunch with me. His dad took a moment to pull me to the side and asked, "David had a mediocre horse today and made a mediocre ride. Why did you single him out in the bronc riding?" I told him that I'd sat back behind the chutes and had watched David get ready to ride. He prepared like a professional, he knew what he was doing. He wasn't just there to be there, he was there to compete and to win. He knew how to prepare, how to set his saddle, he did everything right on the ground. He stretched and warmed up like he should have, set his saddle, measured his rein; he did all the things a pro would do in attempts to achieve perfection. Ultimately, David came to Odessa and competed for me.

I watched those kids and you could tell the ones who are going to do something, who stand out, who have the try. I can watch a guy get ready behind the chutes all day, but if the gate opens and he looks at the ground that's not what I'm looking for. There are really three things I try and look for. Number one, if they have some natural ability then that's always great and a bonus. Number two, their attitude. Are they respectful, are they going to be coachable, what's their demeanor like? Do they show respect to authority? If they give me the time of day and are clearly appreciative about the fact that I've come to see them and they can carry on a conversation with me, that's the kind of kid I wanted. Number three, I liked to see them around their parents and visit with them and their parents. You could get a handle real quick on how they've been parented. I didn't just want kids that are winners and nothing else; I wanted good students and good people. That was very important to me.

Whenever I brought recruits to campus and showed them around, people would always comment later how respectful and well mannered they were. That was the reason they were there though, had they not acted like that then they wouldn't have even been invited. You make a mistake every now and then and get a kid who isn't that way or changes, but they don't last long. They eliminate themselves pretty quickly.

I had a young man one year and it was pretty early in the season. All the kids on my team know what my expectations are, what my rules are, and how I expect them to conduct themselves. No drinking at practice or at the rodeo, if I ever caught you showing up to compete and you'd been drinking you were done! We were putting on our rodeo here at Odessa and I had a schedule so everyone knew what hours they were supposed to work and what events. I made everyone on the team wear their Odessa College vests when they work; it's just professional to do and helps associate good behavior back to the college. This kid showed up and he could barely walk he was so intoxicated and he was supposed to compete the next day.

I walked up to the kid, asked him to give me his vest, and told him to go home. I sent him home right then, he never competed a single time that semester. Fifteen years later, I was out mowing the front yard in the middle of summer, and this kid pulls up in my driveway. He has his wife and his son with him. He got out and walked up to me; I recognized him right off the bat. He asked if I remembered him, which I acknowledged that I did, "Sir, I just wanted to come tell you thank you. You made a man out of me that day; I realized I'd really messed up. Every time I go to do something wrong, I think back about that day and it's changed my whole life."

Another time we were at Big Spring at the college rodeo and I had a young man that was doing well in the region. There were two rodeos left and he had a strong chance at going to the College Finals. He'd done well in the long-go and was making the short-go. He'd made the choice to go out with a bunch of guys the day of the short-go. That night he showed back up to the short-go and I could tell he'd been drinking. It was obvious to me and probably a few other people. He rode out there, nodded his head, and almost instantly fell off his horse.

I just walked away from behind the chutes, I'd helped him get out and all. I met him at the end of the arena. I waited there by the out gate. I told him to give me his vest and that he was done. He looked at me and asked, "Do what? What for?" I told him that he knew exactly what for, he knew the rules. He handed me his vest and that was that.

The next day he came to my office and I told him he was done for the season. He launched into protest about the last rodeo at Tarleton State the next weekend. I just flat out told him he wasn't going. The day after that he slunk back to my office and said," I know you're right, I don't like it but I know you're right. I messed up." I just explained that I couldn't bend the rules just because he had a real shot at College Finals.

He'd known the rules and how firmly I held the team to them. He had made the decision to show up intoxicated and he had to live with the consequences for that. He left Odessa after that semester. About fifteen years later the same situation occurred. He called me up and told me the same thing, "I learned a lot from that. I respect you having the integrity to stick by it."

When Odessa's rodeo team moved facilities from the Watkins Arena to the new team grounds I had a consequence for anyone that broke the rules. If any of my kids got in trouble on any level, even if it wasn't at a college function, and I found out about it, they had to come and pick up rocks around the new facility. They were representing Odessa College, our name, and my name, so there had to be consequences. I'd take the skid steer and drive it out in the middle of any given pen, and tell them when the bucket was full to come and get me and I'd empty it. So they'd spend the day out in the Texas sun picking up rocks out of the pens and the arena. We had rock piles as big as a house from kids breaking the rules.

One night they'd had a party and a bunch of softball girls had gone to the party. Well they all got in trouble for drinking so my rodeo team members were out there picking up rocks the next day. The coach of the softball team called me up and asked if his girls could come over and do the same. He brought 11 girls over and they picked up rocks with my rodeo team kids for four hours. Those kids remember that quite well.

Some people learned from it, some didn't, but that's just the way it was.

I've been to hospitals for surgeries, attended weddings, and gotten phone calls. I've been in the arena when guys have been hurt and killed and luckily none of my kids were part of that. Jerome Davis is the only one of my past students who was seriously injured, but his attitude is untouchable. He and Tiffany both are the most positive, supportive people. He's 110% all the time. When Jerome got hurt he could have easily walked away from the sport forever, but he didn't. He never gave up on his passion for it.

Once my wife and I were headed up to Virginia to see my son who is high ranking in the Navy. On the way we stopped at Jerome and Tiff's house. They were down at the arena so we just drove on down there. Jerome was sitting on his four-wheeler and they were down there trimming some bull's feet. This bull was raising all kinds of trouble. Here I am in a pair of sandals, cut-off shorts, and a polo shirt and I just hop over the railing to go help. This guy was there, he'd been a dairy farmer but was getting into bulls with Jerome's help. He looked at me like I was crazy. I think Jerome read his mind because he just looked at the guy and said, "Don't worry, he knows what he's doing!" I sure didn't look the part when I hopped over the fence, I can admit that! Jerome sure got a kick out of that.

Coaching was such an important part of my life. The relationships I've developed with these kids have been a rewarding part of my life. I've had some exceptional young men and women come through this program and be successful in life. Some kids go on and I don't hear from them again. Some have grown into adults and they still call me and ask me for advice whether it's rodeo related advice or life advice. It's just been so rewarding and I couldn't be more blessed. Coaching the Odessa College Rodeo Team was a very rewarding experience for 25 years.

Buddy Hawkins

Team roper Buddy Hawkins was born in Sedan, Kansas but now calls Columbus, Kansas home. Buddy married his wife Krista in 2006.

Both Buddy's parents were involved in rodeo, his mom ran barrels and breakaway roped while his dad competed in tie-down and team roping events. Some of Buddy's first memories were of rodeo, traveling across the country and watching his parents compete.

Buddy didn't pick up roping until the fall of 2000. He started competing in 2001, and in 2002 he won his first check. In the Spring of 2004 Buddy's career began to take off, slowly building and improving leading him to win three trucks in 2008.

In 2009 Buddy bought his PRCA permit and at 23 began climbing the ranks of the professional rodeo circuit. 2010 prompted Buddy to buy his permit again and he faced a tough year. Buddy decided to take 2011 off to train some young horses and allow himself to prepare more.

2012 would be Buddy's rookie year in the PRCA. He qualified for San Antonio and finished in the Top 45. 2013 brought wins at San Antonio, Nampa, and a trip to the Wrangler National Finals where Buddy won a go-round.

In 2014 Buddy won the Odessa Sand Hills Jackpot, the Fort Worth Stock Show & Rodeo, the Bob Feist Invitational, and qualified for RFD-TV's The American.

Buddy finished out the 2014 season winning Reserve Championship at the United States Team Roping Open Tour and finishing just outside of the Top 30 in the world.

"If you want to be successful like you want to breathe, then you'll be successful."

"Humble Beginnings"

The beginning of my roping career is different for me than it is most other guys; I got a later start to things. I was around rodeo some when I was little but I was interested in other things.

In the fall of 1999 we moved back to Sedan where my uncle was starting horses. At the same time my dad got back into team roping. My uncle would call me, I was 13 or 14, and I'd go trail ride with him or whatever he asked to help get his young horses some exposure. I didn't really know what I was doing, but he'd pick me up and off we'd go.

I already knew how to swing a rope so I started messing around with the steers he had, just kind of goofing off. I'd actually been spending years learning and practicing the violin. My predominate focus at that time was being a violinist and music. I wanted that to be my career actually.

My violin teacher was actually in Wichita, Kansas so we'd go over there for my lessons and we'd see some family. Eventually, it became more and more challenging to make that trip. We were on a limited budget so the 100-mile trip was starting to add up.

My dad was going to jackpot team ropings all over. I remember being 13 years old, going to those ropings, and I'd watch and listen. I'd hear how roping would pay out, though to some it might not see like a lot; $119 here, $63 there, whatever the numbers were. For a kid who didn't have a lot of means, living in the country, with basically no opportunities to work for anything more than minimum wage, it caught my attention. It fascinated me; I saw how people could make significantly more money than I had at the time.

Spring of 2001 I actually had the opportunity to start practicing roping on a bit more serious level. Seemingly overnight, after watching those ropings, I decided that's what I wanted to do. I considered it for a while, my music was unnatural for me, I was skilled because I worked at it everyday. I wasn't gifted though; music wasn't an easy thing for me to do. I had even less skill when it came to roping, but my dad helped me try to figure it out. It was all pretty hard for me but I started noticing small improvements. I could see the light at the end of the tunnel.

So at 15 I got my hands on every available form of media that I could, usually VHS tapes. But if anyone had a team roping video or magazine, whatever was accessible, I was consuming whatever knowledge I could. I studied the pictures, I studied the images, I watched those VHS tapes in slow motion for hours. I watched how they rode, how they roped, headers, heelers, I studied every little movement those guys made.

I really started breaking it down. I'm an analytical person by nature so stuff started making sense and my roping seemed to click a little bit more. The force of the loop, angle of the swing, these details made sense to me. In 2002 I was still super green but I started understanding. I could imitate those guys sure, but I needed to figure out why they did what they did. Ultimately that was going to make me better.

By 2003 things were clicking a bit more but I was on green horses that didn't know what they were doing and I didn't know what I was doing. The partners I had weren't clicking, and there were just a lot of inconsistencies. I hadn't gotten any professional advice or training, everything was all secondhand and not necessarily relevant to the time. My mind was really weak too. I did have an opportunity for success but I couldn't handle the pressure. I studied the sports psychology of athletes from all sports, trying to learn how these guys mentally handled things when the pressure was on.

In 2004 I made a run and it all just clicked. It was the first time I had ever really seen and experienced what was going on. I saw the feet, I felt my horse keyed into things, and I placed my loop in a way that would later become my predominant loop placement. I remember all the details of that run; the sun, my horse, the way the rope felt in my hand, everything about that one run. I just started trying to recreate that feeling.

I quit worrying about the time factor of my runs and just started trying to focus on my swing, my timing, and delivery. I started getting better and better and was able to create that same feeling more and more. It was 5 out of 10 times, then 7 out of 10 times, then 9 out of 10 times. I got to where I could do it with a high level of consistency and a low level of competition.

I started going to jackpots and continued accomplishing things. I wasn't competitive at the big ropings though. I could go to the little rodeo and be competitive, but at the bigger ones my mind was still interfering. I felt like I needed to do something different at the bigger rodeos than I did at the smaller jackpots and it would mess with my head. I'd beat myself 9 out of 10 times. That continued through 2005 and 2006. Once I started getting out of my own head, things started to turn around and I could see progress.

When it came time for me to move up in the ranks of professional rodeo, I didn't have the option or means to acquire a horse that was "pro rodeo ready" so I had to learn to train green horses or horses that might not be as talented as others. I had to hunt around to find the type of horses I needed, they didn't just fall in my lap. The process was a bit tedious at times but ultimately it was rewarding. I've made every horse I've had; I've only bought one horse. I've either had colts that weren't broke to ride or they were broke but they'd never been roped on.

There are so many aspects to every sport, especially team roping. Horsemanship, roping ability, and being at the right place mentally. Every level of competition has guys who's minds fail them more often than not. Your mental game has to be just as strong and your physical game. That's something I've educated myself on as I have progressed. I try to focus on staying mentally aware; I'm getting better at it. You can't physically develop a good mental game but you can mentally develop a good physical game; it's mind over matter. During the past five or six years, it's just been a concentration on those things; better horsemanship, better roping, and maintaining a better mindset.

I set a lifelong goal to be a professional team roper. To this day, I've probably set thousands of goals I wanted to accomplish, but to this day as far as rodeo is concerned, that's still my goal; to make a living team roping. I want to win world championships, but my goal is to make a living doing what I love to do. That's why I get up and do it everyday.

The best advice I've ever been given is to get up and go to work everyday. I look forward to a new week. I look forward to getting up and going to do what I love and putting in the effort to be successful. If you work towards your passion, towards whatever you want, that's a true sense of accomplishment. No great relationships, whether it's your relationship with Christ, or your relationship in marriage, are easy and really great accomplishments are never easy. If relationships were easy then everybody would be successful in them.

The most challenging things are the most rewarding things. You have to put yourself outside of your comfort zone and go to work. There's actually a lyric in a Nelly song that says, "If hard work pays off then easy work is worthless", I think that's exactly right. So if I have to get up and go to work everyday, I believe we reap what we sow. I'm glad I have the opportunity to do that. I'm only going to be as good as I push myself to be. If you're training everyday, hard training, then you're going to reap a harvest in that area of your life. But on the flip side of that, we can't always dictate everything. Things happen, bad calves, bad steers, lame horses. You just have to keep putting in the work and know it's going to pay off in the long run.

In rodeo especially, there can be major dry spells between pay-offs; days, months, years. I've tried to almost back myself down to where it's almost not about the win but about the improvement. The pursuit of perfection is a driving force; you strive for that, and it is the motivation behind what I do. You just have to get up and go to work everyday.

Kirsten Vold

Kirsten Vold was born and raised on the rodeo road by her stock contracting father and her trick-riding mother. Born at a rodeo in El Paso, Texas it's ironic to say she was introduced to rodeo at a young ago. Home schooled until she was a freshmen in high school, Kirsten's early life was wrapped up in rodeo and going from one rodeo to the next.

Kirsten basically lived at home alone from her sophomore year in high school until her graduation. Since her family was on the road most of the year, ranch hands and help would keep an eye on her so her family wouldn't have to worry.

Kirsten started at Tarleton State University, but went on to graduate from the University of Southern Colorado (now Colorado State University-Pueblo) with a BA in Communications and initially took up a job in sports marketing and promotion. Kirsten took a job with a company that did licensing for the PBR, PRCA, and AQHA, a position that allowed her to have the corporate life she thought she wanted and still use her rodeo connections.

"I liked rodeo, but I didn't think it was what I was going to do. I was going to be a lawyer and drive a sports car and live in L.A. I thought rodeo was good, but I just thought there was a lot more out there."

Kirsten missed being around the animals and missed the ranch so she chose to return home. While she was home Kirsten briefly worked for a record company in New York City helping create a compilation of rodeo songs to make an official PRCA album.

Kirsten Vold began managing her father's company, Harry Vold Rodeo Company, in the spring of 1997 when she was just 25. Her determination, work ethic, and honesty eventually won over her critics and she's only continued to exceed their expectations.

One of Kirsten's greatest achievements is her stud horse Painted Valley. Painted Valley was selected for six Wrangler National Finals Rodeos, voted Best Saddle Bronc Horse of the WNFR in 2009, and was named the 2010 PRCA Saddle Bronc Horse of the Year.

Today Kirsten makes her home in Colorado and oversees one of the most fa-mous rodeo stock companies in the industry today. Kirsten in a trusted indus-try veteran and her family's company sets the standard by which all others are measured.

"Changes"

The first year I came back to be part of the company was a year when I learned a lot. Initially, I was put in a foreman position, general manager I guess you could say, of the company. That wasn't an easy thing to do. You have guys that are older than you or people in general that are older than you that not only felt more experienced but actually were more experienced; now they had to take orders from a 25 year old female. The ones I probably ran into the most trouble with were the guys who I'd par-tied with in college with or grew up with. Having them learn to see me in a position of authority versus the "buddy" role was a tough adjustment. The first year or two was a bit rocky.

I've never thought my gender was an issue. I probably think it's less of an issue than it actually is. We had a couple people quit and then want to come back and finally I just had to set some boundaries. It was hard to do. I was 25 or 26 and these were people I'd known for awhile. I had relationships with them so it was just a year or two of adjustment.

Rodeo cowboys have such a short career, especially in the rough-stock world. I'm basically on the 3rd generation of riders. There were people competing when I was a kid and now they're rodeo coaches and their kids are competing. Then there were the guys I grew up with and now their kids are riding. Like Cody Wright, I was there when he won the College Finals and he was such a big deal; now I'm putting his son on my broncs. It's so weird but so cool; it's one of the best parts of my job. It just seems to fly by. Cody has five kids now but he's still very competitive riding broncs.

This year Cody DeMers and I were talking about the old times. He and Cody Wright had traveled together and stayed with me when they competed at the Colorado State Fair. One time the yard guy had shown up to mow the grass. He'd come to the door to get paid and Cody DeMers and Cody Wright were sitting on my couch in the middle of the afternoon waiting for the rodeo to start. I answered the door and paid the guy, he looked over my shoulder and said, "Must be nice to have your mom pay someone to mow the grass while you lay on the couch."

Cody DeMers has been telling that story for years and it came up again this year at Houston. We realized that had happened 15 years ago; you just loose all track of time, time just goes on. Here these guys are either wrapping up their career or retiring and I'm doing the same thing. Probably the hardest thing for me to realize is that I'm getting older, because I stay around people who are the same age. They may age out of the system but new kids fill their places and we all still have the same things in common and talk about the same things. Sometimes I have to remind myself that I'm not 26 anymore! But every once in a while one of those kids will say something and I just think, "Oh yeah, you're 24…"

It's good though; I enjoy the fact that I get to be there to share people's great moments with them. Some of the most important and exciting moments like winning world championships for the first time or the third time, or you get to be there when they win the College National Finals, or you're there when their son wins. I just think, "What a great occupation, to be there when so many people are on an adrenaline rush and have such monumentally important things happen to them".

If you talk to anyone about rodeo I bet they all say the same thing, whether it's Roy Cooper who's retired or Tuf Cooper who's just at the peak of his career; it's that the people in this industry are the best part about it. The miles get long. It's hard to get fired up about driving 2,000 miles when you just missed your calf or got bucked off. You have to climb back in a car and have to drive 1,000 or 2,000 miles to do the same thing. When you're hurt and competing, or you haven't won anything in a month and the bills are piling up, those are all things these guys deal with on a daily basis.

You don't make a lot of money in rodeo, so the reason we do this is probably because of this bond you share with people that I just don't find in other fields of work. I've been in other fields of work and there are a lot of great people all over, but there's a certain bond in the rodeo world.

After the short-go in Dodge City this year, a brawl broke out at the beer stand and it's kind of funny because everyone is jumping in to defend their buddy or their brother. I'm sure that happens in other spots, but there's a level of respect here that's special. There's just really good people. It's like any other industry, there's shady stuff that goes on and people you don't like but overall it's just a good group of people.

People always ask me about famous cowboys I know, but they're not famous people to me. Those guys are just another cowboy to me or they are my friends. Growing up I was around guys that were "famous" but I never saw them that way. They're just people like you and me. Sid Steiner said one time, "Our world is so small compared to other sports" and he's right. When you're in it you really feel like you're a big deal but rodeo is actually a very small world. It's really easy to be "famous" in the rodeo world because you're not competing with the number of athletes that are in something like the NFL. Fame can happen FAST, it doesn't take long for everyone to know about you.

Lane Frost was famous just because everyone liked being around him. That's one of the reasons he became so well known. He never was too busy to sign an autograph or talk to a kid. Cowboys today need to remember they were once those kids without any patches on their shirts, asking their heroes for just a minute of their time. But I understand when guys head out to Las Vegas to the NFR and they're being fawned over wherever they go. It's hard to not let that go to your head. The reality of it though is that you're still just a person. Taylor Swift can't just stop at a Walmart and go shopping, but Trevor Brazile can stop at any Walmart anywhere in America. He can throw on a hat and sunglasses and be himself, which I'm sure he probably enjoys.

I just love working behind the scenes of a rodeo. But beyond that, the volunteers and rodeo committee members don't get the credit they truly deserve. You have to have people who want those jobs or the rodeos don't happen. People to organize the event, put up prize money, make up rodeo committees, do the paperwork, and answer phones. Without those people doing jobs that may seem meaningless to others, we wouldn't even have a sport. They're probably the least recognized people in our sport and absolutely the most important. If they didn't show up to their jobs, then I wouldn't have a job. People so often seem to forget about these people, contestants included.

Sometimes contestants do not understand the importance of the rodeo committee. You can't yell at the guy working the gate or march up to the head of the committee and complain about the stock. You have to go in and offer to help. It's very rare to hear a cowboy offer to do a TV or media plug for a rodeo, and rodeos can't keep going without that kind of promotion. I've seen committee members approach cowboys about signing autographs after the rodeo and they either blow them off or they don't show up to sign for an hour; it would help them as individuals and their sport so much. You have to show up for your sport and your fans. You shouldn't have to be paid to do that. There's a handful that do, I'm not knocking everyone, but that handful needs to grow.

Probably the most difficult thing or the biggest obstacle I find is the fact that it's hard to find good people to work for you, good, solid help. I remember when Dad almost quit the business and sold out because he was so frustrated with his crew. At that time I couldn't understand it. I didn't understand how you could be the boss and your help could drive you to that point. I definitely understand that now. It's hard to find good people and rarely anyone is going to care as much as you do.

We pride ourselves on having a crew that likes to do what they do. We all enjoy working together and we've had some really solid crews. But it just takes one person to throw the whole team off. Sometimes it's just not just fun, it's a job and you have to restructure and make changes. You have to hire people on a full-time basis; people don't want to work a part-time, seasonal job where they have to find additional work in the off-season and this can be a very physically demanding job.

There are more people behind the scenes than people realize. To make it work you have to be able to have people at the ranch, driving trucks, and keeping up with the books. It'd be easier to do it by yourself, because you know all the different aspects of things, but you can't do it by yourself. In the off-season I can take on more by myself, but when things are going full steam ahead it's impossible. You have to have good help that you trust and you know they're going to show up, and you want it to be fun.

Our industry and our sport are changing a lot; some changes are good and some changes are bad. Money is becoming more of an issue. Starting with the 2015 National Finals they're almost doubling the money the stock contractors and contestants will be making; that's good. That show the sport is making progress and allows it to grow. Unfortunately, it doesn't bring out the best in people. Anytime you bring in more money you'll see people do things you thought they'd never do; they'll do those things for more money. It's almost too bad because you almost don't want the positive changes because you don't want to deal with the negative repercussions that are going to follow the changes. That's just growth though.

My dad is 90 years old and so much has changed since he starting in this business, especially in the last 10-15 years. It's hard for him to understand how much the business has changed and how quickly. It's an ever-changing sport. You either have to change with it or you have to bow out. You can't stay the same and stay competitive. I have to change things that have always worked for him in the past and he'll say, "Well that's the way we've always done things!" It just doesn't work that way now so we go round and round. Feed and personnel are probably the two biggest issues. I believe in finding good people and paying them well. If they don't do their job then you just get rid of them. Dad has never fired somebody in his life! I guess I'm more cut and dry about that. The bar is set and you either rise to meet it or you're gone.

I have great friends in this business though, great friends. I feel very fortunate that I get to enjoy a job and work a job that consistently puts me around these people. I don't think my gender has played a huge role in what I do. I think you do what you want to do because you want to do it. I wasn't trying to break down any "gender roles" when I started, I just loved the animals and the sport. People may be harder on me because I'm a girl, but those people don't really expect a lot sometimes so whenever you do something halfway good they're shocked and amazed. If I were Harry Vold's son they'd expect me to be able to do this stuff. So in that regard, I think being a girl has probably actually made things easier on me in most aspects.

You can't really dwell on it when someone does make a dig at your gender. If you do, then you become them. Because I'm a girl I shouldn't be able to know this or know that, guys who are half my age will challenge some things I say. I don't even really acknowledge it. I pick up on it and I know why it is, but I don't acknowledge the reasoning behind it because I don't believe in it. It is what you make it. If you make something a bigger deal than what it is then other people are just going to follow suit. There's no use in building a mountain out of a molehill. I don't acknowledge that it's different when I'm back behind the chutes and guys are changing clothes and taping up. I think sometimes they forget I am actually a girl!

I know that there is sexism and I know that it goes on. There are competitors of my Dad who are just waiting to move in and try to buy this business from me when he's gone. Would they be quite so apt to do that if I was a guy? Probably not. Will they use that as their sales pitch when they're going after rodeo committees? Some of them will probably try it. That's where I have to let my reputation precede me and not acknowledge it. I can't change I'm a girl so I chose not to recognize it as an issue. I just want to go forward with my business and allow my stock and my work to speak for themselves.

People will say things to me sometimes and I know they mean them as a compliment but that's not always how they come across. One of my first years in Fort Worth I was behind the chutes and this older volunteer was trying to help me load my stock. They let them do that there, but I don't like anyone handling my stock that I don't know. I always just kind of jumped in ahead of them and did it myself. So I just told this guy to let me know where he wanted the stock to go and I moved them around. When we were done he went, "I've never worked with a girl before, you're pretty good!" You can't do anything but just shake that off and know that he's trying to pay you a compliment and move forward.

This past year at the College Finals a kid's parent was parked back where we move livestock and such. He'd be watching me work for a few days and finally this dad comes up to me and goes, "I want you to know I think you do a good job. I don't know another woman that could do this job!" I know he probably knows a lot of other men who could do this job, but because I'm a woman he felt the need to say something about it. Again, I know he meant it as a compliment but they're more or less backhanded compliments. I just thanked him and chuckled a bit; no need to make that a big deal or let it get to me. Stuff like that is funny to me. It can't offend you. You just have to shake it off and keep working.

A lot of women in this industry are barrel racers or rodeo secretaries. But it's slowly changing and that's another area of positive change. Sometimes you have to go out of your comfort zone for change, but it's usually worth it.

Sage Kimzey

Sage Kimzey hails from Strong City, Oklahoma.

Sage's family has deep roots in the rodeo world; his father Ted was a longtime PRCA barrelman while his mom, older sister, and younger brother make up the professional trick-riding group, Tricked Out.

Sage attends Southwestern Oklahoma State University where he's majoring in Business. After bull riding, Sage plans to return to his family's ranch and go into the cattle business.

Sage currently rides bulls in both the PRCA and CBR and headed to the 2014 National Finals #1 in the world.

Sage would go on to be crowned the 2014 Resistol Rookie of the Year, win Rounds 3, 4, 7, and 9 at the 2014 National Finals, win the 2014 NFR average, and ultimately win the 2014 World Champion Bull Rider.

Sage is the first bull rider since 1963 to win both Rookie of the Year and be crowned World Champion in the same year.

"U-Stuck"

Brennon Eldred and I flew down to Houston, Texas for a Championship Bull Riding (CBR) event in Conroe, Texas. We had arranged to have some friends pick us up from the airport and take us to the CBR event. Neither Brennon nor I are old enough to rent a car yet, so we were really relying on our friends to get us around.

We were sitting outside the Houston airport and we were waiting and waiting…and waiting. Finally our ride called us. Turns out they'd gotten about five miles from the airport and the whole interstate had been locked down. There was no way they were going to get to us anytime soon, much less get us to the event on time.

Brennon and I immediately started panicking; our options to get to the CBR were slim to none. We couldn't rent a car, and our ride was stuck in a gridlock!

As I was standing there wracking my brain I remember my dad

telling me that if I ever got in a pinch that we could rent a U-Haul van. He'd told me you only have to be an 18 year old to rent a U-Haul.

I turned to Brennon and said, "If we don't have a ride we're going to have to go rent a U-Haul van. That's going to be the only way for us to make it at this point." Brennon just looked and me and said, "Well let's do it."

The hotel we'd stayed at actually had a shuttle that would take you anywhere in a 3 mile radius for free. We took the shuttle service and made the arrangements.

"Where would you like to go, sir?"

"The U-Haul place, it says it's only 2.6 miles from here."

"Ummm okay…we'll be ready for you momentarily."

So the shuttle took us to the U-haul place and we walked up to the rental desk. The guy behind the desk immediately launched into twenty questions of where were we moving our stuff, how much stuff did we have to move, on and on.

"Well sir, we just need a van. Pretty much the cheapest thing you can rent us will do. There are just two of us."

"Well son, what are you boys moving?"

"We're not really moving anything, sir. We can bring the van back tonight, no problem."

Brennon and I just told the man we had to take a few things up to Conroe, which we did. We had to take our gear bags and ourselves to a rodeo; we figured that counted as moving something.

"How old are you boys anyways?"

"We're both 20, sir."

Seemingly hesitantly they rented us their cheapest U-Haul van and off we went. We pushed that U-Haul van to the max 60mph speed it allowed and managed to pull into the bull riding just as it was starting.

We both rode great and ended up in the money. We drove back that night, turned the U-Haul in with some dirt in the floorboard, and went back to the hotel. Sometimes you've just got to pull a MacGyver and make something work for you when it seems like you don't have any other options.

Kenny Bergeron

Kenny Bergeon hails from Eunice, Louisiana but calls Mowata, Louisiana home.

Kenny was just 15 when he stepped into an arena, took his first hooking, and instantly took to bull fighting. Kenny began fighting bulls professionally in 2001. Kenny's dad and uncle were both stock contractors and his dad fought bulls when Kenny was a kid.

The south Louisiana bullfighter has been nominated as the Professional Rodeo Cowboys Association Bullfighter of the Year every year since 2008. In that time, he's been chosen by the bull riders to protect them during the Wrangler National Finals Rodeo in both 2010 and 2011. Kenny has worked the Texas Circuit Finals seven years in a row.

When he's not fighting bulls and protecting cowboys Kenny is the proud, full-time dad of two kids. Kenny does some welding on the side, but rodeo is his passion.

"Reality TV"

We were in Lafayette a few years ago; Travis Adams and I were fighting bulls. (Travis fought bulls at the NFR in 2006). Travis has been my mentor; I owe a lot of my pro rodeo career to him. Without him I probably wouldn't have made it. He made sure I made the connections I needed to, got my jobs when I was starting out, and has become one of my best friends in rodeo.

Lafayette is in mid-January so it's kind of the first rodeo of the year after the NFR. Everybody has been off for a couple weeks; they're getting over the NFR hangover, so when they come to Lafayette the party is on. South Louisiana is my hometown rodeo. I know a lot of people and it's one of the few opportunities for hometown people to see me fight bulls.

Bars in Lafayette don't close; as long as someone is buying drinks they'll stay open. You can imagine if the rodeo starts on a Thursday and ends on a Sunday, the party is nonstop. Well also in Lafayette, since it's my hometown, we have to do a lot of TV appearances to talk about rodeo and bullfighting. They go on the morning show at the local news station two or three times, newspaper articles, etc.

After the rodeo on Friday night, Travis and I headed to the bar. It's a big ol' time and the bar is just packed. We had to be on TV at 6 o'clock the next morning to talk up the rodeo. We're pretty good at drinking and partying and then doing what we have to do the next day; we figured we'd get some sleep in there sometime. Waking up early the next morning after a night at the bar isn't that big of a deal; we do it all the time.

We drink it up pretty good and party it up pretty hard. Before we know it, it's 5am and we have to be on TV in an hour. Travis looks at me and goes, "Holy shit, we have to be on TV at 6 am." We were some kind of tore up.

From the bar to the arena is about four or five miles through downtown Lafayette. The population is only about 100,000 people so traffic isn't too terrible. For some reason I had driven to the bar and for some reason I decided I would drive and get us back to the arena where my camper was. We got in my truck and got back to the arena, and Travis is so drunk he doesn't even get out of my truck. He just told me, "Come wake me up when it's time to go, I'm sleeping right here." I went in my camper and passed out in the same clothes I went to the bar in.

At 5:30 am, which was about 20 minutes later, Travis comes banging on my camper door, "Hey, we've got to go. We're late, get up, we've got to go." I just looked at him with one eye open, "I quit. Tell them whatever you need to, I'll take care of it later, I quit." Travis just kept pestering me, "No, you're not quitting. Get up right now, get your shit together." Finally I realized he wasn't going to shut up and go away so I shuffled out of the trailer and off we went to the TV station. Travis and I are still drunk as can be, but we hopped in the truck and took off.

Lecile Harris was the clown at the rodeo and he was going to be on the morning show as well. Lecile is almost like a grandfather to us. He's been around rodeo forever, mentored us along, and we're really close. Lecile already had his mic on and was on the couch waiting for us. We were 30 minutes late to do this interview. We're still in the same clothes we wore to the bar, smelling like cigarettes and god knows what else. We're walking past people in the station and they're looking at us like we're the walking dead.

I sat on Lecile's left hand side and Travis plopped down on his right hand side. Lecile looked at me, then slowly turned and looked at Travis. This grin crept over his face and he goes, "You two bastards are drunk aren't you?" I just looked at him, "Yes sir, yes sir we are." Lecile knew us long enough to know how we rolled and he thought it was hysterical.

So the news reporter comes over and sits in a chair across from us to do the interview. He asked me a question and I just responded, "Yeah". He paused, looked at me and then asked Travis a question to which Travis also responded with one-word, "Yeah". He didn't ask us any more questions after that and Lecile just took over the interview, which Lecile loved.

Since it's my hometown a lot of people watch the morning show and they were all texting and calling me and telling me how good I had been. I was like, "Yeah, I'm sure I was just amazing." I know I was all glassy eyed and looked like shit! I can't say that was the first time that ever happened, probably won't be the last time either.

"Raise 'Em Up"

At the 2011 National Finals Rodeo, I was nominated for Bullfighter of The Year and had also been selected to fight bulls during the performances as well. Since I was doing both, my whole family came to Las Vegas; dad, dad's girlfriend, and my daughter Addison came to the awards banquet with me.

I should preface this story by stating that I'm from south Louisiana; we drink. We're not shy about it, it's just part of the culture and it's just the way it is. It's also nothing if you're drinking a beer, and your kid wants a sip, to give them a sip. I'm not saying I let her sit there and drink a six-pack with me. But if Addison wants a sip of beer, it's nothing to hand her the bottle and let her have a sip of beer.

Anyways, we're up there at the awards banquet and the room is filled with people. My dad has just had both knees replaced so he wasn't getting around too well. By the time we got up to the room where they were having the cocktail party he'd walked a bit and his knees were bothering him. Before the banquet I'd sent Addison to the salon to get her hair done, bought her a dress, and done everything I could to make her feel special and feel like a princess.

There's probably 3,000 people in this room and it is super crowded. I told my dad to sit at the table and I'd wade through the crowd to the bar and bring drinks back to the table. I told Addison to stay with him and I'd be right back. I head to the bar and I get about 50 feet into the madness and about 1,000 people deep, turn around and Addison is right behind me. I wasn't going to wade back through all those people to take her back so I just grabbed her hand and brought her with me.

We finally got to the bar, I ordered two whiskey drinks and got myself a beer. There was a lot of handshaking, back slapping politicking going on up there so it took awhile. Finally we started making our way back to the table, but people keep stopping me and it's just taking forever. Addison starts chiming up that she's thirsty; I'm trying to explain to her that as soon as I get these drinks back to the table I'll go back to the bar and get her a soda or something.

We shuffled through a couple more people and she starts back up with how thirsty she is, so I just handed her my beer. "Here, take a sip of this." Well she freaking turns that bottle up and makes it bubble, straight up cocks it back. So here's this 5-year-old, head full of curls and wearing a princess dress, with a Coors Light straight kicked up like she knows what she's doing.

Some people looked horrified, but most everyone started laughing at her. She finishes and hands it back to me, I just turned to everyone and said, "She's from south Louisiana, it isn't her first beer!" Everyone just busted out laughing and we just headed right on back to our table.

JB Mauney

North Carolina's JB Mauney first began riding sheep at age three, he moved on to steers by age nine, and his first bull at age 13. It's been history ever since.

His first Professional Bull Rider's Built Ford Tough Series event was in 2006 and he was crowned the Daisy Rookie of the Year that same year. In addition to the PBR, JB competed in Championship Bull Riding (CBR) and qualified for the CBR Finals in 2005 and 2006. He briefly competed on the PRCA circuit from 2009-2011.

JB joined the PBR full time in 2007 and finished 3rd in the world that year. In 2008 and 2009 he would finish 2nd in the world finals. However, in 2009 JB set a record by becoming the first cowboy in PBR history to ride all eight bulls at the PBR Finals.

JB has qualified for every PBR Finals since 2007 and has been awarded the Lane Frost/Brent Thurman Award three times (2007, 2008, 2009). JB is also the only cowboy to ever cover the legendary Bushwacker, the 2011 and 2014 PBR Bull of the Year. He is also well known for being the only rider to ride both Bones, the 2008 and 2010 PBR Bull of the year, Code Blue, the 2009 PBR Bull of the Year, and Asteroid, the 2012 PBR Bull of the Year.

In 2013 JB reached the pinnacle of his sport and was crowned the 2013 Professional Bull Riders World Champion.

Today JB makes his home outside Mooresville, NC with his wife, Lexie, and their daughter, Bella.

"Onto The Next One"

One year, I think it was 2010, I had a collapsed lung and had been home for most of the summer. I'd just gotten healed up and was ready to get back at it so we headed to Salinas, Texas. After Salinas we headed to Tulsa, Oklahoma and from there we went to Cheyenne. The following Monday and Tuesday we moved on to Livingston, Montana, and then on Wednesday to Yuba City, California. To end the week, on Thursday I flew back to Texas and on Friday, I was entered up in Weatherford that night.

When I landed in Fort Worth they called and told me what two bulls I'd drawn. I was really excited about them. But landing around 5pm in Fort Worth means one thing, traffic. I'd seen Cody Campbell at the airport and he jumped in the car with me. We were driving down the shoulder of the highway, passing cars on the right side, passing cars on the left side; anyway we could go to get there. I'd drawn good bulls and I wanted to ride them.

Luckily they didn't give our bulls away or turn them out. I don't know how, but we managed to get there just as the first section was starting. That was the section we both just happened to be riding in. We jumped out of the car and threw on our gear as fast as we could.

The two bulls I was in a hurry to get on proved to not be so good. One of them flipped over on me in the bucking chute and the other one fell down about four seconds into my ride and rolled over on top of me. I ended up having two re-ride bulls, which got me back to the short round. So all week long I was in a hurry to get back just to get on two bulls and I ended up getting on five.

So after five bulls, I climbed back in the car, drove all night, and rode in San Antonio the next night. It was an epic rodeo run. I used to move around like that, but not anymore.

"Can't Hang"

It was usually Brian Canter, Kasey Hayes, Ty Smith, Ned Cross, and myself; we were about 20 years old and we were just getting going. We were ready to rock n' roll. We had some older guys who climbed in and traveled with us for about two weeks, or should I say tried to travel with us.

The last bull riding they went to with us we pulled in late, like really late.

"Y'all are always running late!"

The older guys just said, "You should travel with these young guys! The past two weeks we've been nothing but late! They don't care whether they get here on time or not!"

Those older guys just couldn't hang with us. They were so worried about being late and with us being younger and a bit wild they almost would worry themselves into a heart attack. We were so kicked back our attitude was, "Oh we'll get there when we get there!"

They just didn't like our style; we were young and wild and didn't care about being places on time. I wish I'd known then what I know now. I'm not sure it would've changed much, but maybe it would have, I don't know.

Cory Wooldridge

Cory Wooldridge was born and raised in Enid, Oklahoma but calls Eaton, Colorado home.

Cory's mom ran barrels and his dad, Virgil Wooldridge, was a bull rider. You could say that Cory was born into the sport of rodeo. Cory rode calves and steers until he was 15 when he made the change to fighting bulls.

When Cory was 22 he decided to get a bronc saddle and climbed aboard his first saddle bronc horse at a local practice pen. Cory instantly fell in love with it and swapped fighting bulls for riding broncs. Cory obtained his PRCA permit and has been committed to the sport every since.

In addition to riding saddle broncs, Cory owns C Bar W Leather, specializing in custom belts, wallets, and other leatherwork.

Cory has a younger brother, Cody, who's a bull rider and a sister, Heidi.

"Put Your Left Hand Out"

We'd headed to Laramie, WY for their rodeo, which takes place in early July before Cheyenne Frontier Days. I was relatively new to the saddle bronc horses, but I just loved it; I was so happy to be riding.

I ended up bucking off and in a moment of pure reaction, when I went to land, I stuck my arm out to brace my fall. When I went to get up I knew it felt weird; my arm felt extra heavy, like it was just dead weight. I looked down and saw that half my arm was pointing in the wrong way!

My dad was off work and had come up to watch us. He was watching me from over besides the chutes so I went jogging over there to show him. As I got closer and people could see my arm, I could hear the entire stand gasp over the contorted appearance of my arm. The bones weren't sticking through the skin, but it was really close.

I got back behind the chutes and I knew right away my arm was broken. I was trying to take my chaps and vest off with one arm and the pain was starting to intensify. As the guys around me saw my arm they all slowly started backing away to give me some space. I distinctly recall one bull rider puking over the sight of it. Those boys weren't handling it very well.

My dad and I waited 15 minutes for the ambulance to show up; why they didn't have one there I don't know. They wanted to give me a ride to the hospital, but I was like, "No, I'm not riding in the ambulance. That's like $3,000 for four blocks!" The EMTs just took some ACE bandage and made a makeshift sling for me. I hopped in the car with my dad and we headed to the Laramie hospital. The problem was that we couldn't find the hospital even though it was like right around the corner. We were in a 1998 Ford Explorer and kept hitting these speed bumps trying to find the hospital entrance. Worst four blocks of my life!

By the time I got to the hospital every nurse, doctor, whatever was sitting outside waiting for me. They had a wheelchair, which I brushed off, "Guys, my legs aren't broken." I thought we were just going to roll in there and get it taken care of, but the doctor told me he wanted to let the swelling go down overnight and then reset it. I laughed, I thought he was joking. Why couldn't they just put me in a cast and send me on my way?

I remember when they took the bandages off so they could take x-rays, half my arm kind of just flopped out on the table, and the nurse made a face and had to turn away so she wouldn't be sick. It was a pretty disgusting sight and sound. They told me I had to stay the night and have surgery in the morning; I didn't have any other option. Turns out I broke two bones in my left arm that required a plate and six screws on each bone.

I was already pretty upset because I'd drawn at Estes Park the next weekend. That was a rodeo I'd really been wanting to get in and I had a great horse drawn. So here I was laying in the Laramie hospital all night long. I've never watched that many episodes of "Two and a Half Men" in my life. That was the only thing on TV worth watching. I couldn't sleep because it felt like someone had a hammer and they were just pounding on my arm all night long. They had me on IV pain meds with a button I could push like every 15 minutes; I couldn't seem to push that button enough.

Next morning they come in my room and whisked me off to surgery. My poor dad had gotten a hotel room in Laramie, and come back to the hospital the next morning before they took me to surgery. The surgery went fine. Pins and screws got put it, and they took me back to my room for recovery.

The Laramie hospital is not really the place to be. The nurse was even honest about that. She was like, "The kitchen's not open and you wouldn't want anything from it even if it was open." She did bring me a Sprite though, and I drank that and laid there for about an hour. I was itching to leave and finally just blatantly asked when I could go. She said the doctor had cleared me so I could go whenever. I asked, "Where's my pants? I'm out of here."

I got dressed and we headed right back to the rodeo. I made it to about the bronc riding and my pain meds started wearing off, then I was ready to go back home.

I was so glad my dad was there, that he'd taken the time off work to be there and stay (and let me go back to the rodeo). I felt like a little kid though, because I totally guilt-tripped him into stopping and buying me a Frosty at Wendy's. I remember he was asking me if I was hungry and I was like, "I could go for an ice cream…like a Frosty maybe?"

That was definitely an experience, and I had to take a year off to let my arm heal and do physical therapy. When I first went back to the surgeon, they took the big cast off, my staples out, and fitted me with a smaller cast. There was a green rod sticking out of my wrist. The doctor informed me that during surgery they'd discovered I'd also dislocated my wrist and shoved the bone forward. I had to live with a rod sticking out of my wrist for two more weeks before they pulled that out.

It's just been a huge process to get the feeling back and build the muscles. Luckily, it was my free arm, except that day. That day I'd decided to ride left-handed, and my ride felt better than any right-handed right I'd made. If I hadn't broken it I would switch hands, but I just know there's no way it could hold up and be as strong as I need it to be.

The first ride back took awhile; I wasn't scared of getting hurt. It was more the mental game of knowing I needed to ride my best so I didn't get hurt again or reinjure what had taken so long to heal. I didn't know if it was going to hurt or what, I just didn't trust it. It took me awhile to feel confident in it again. Even now when I'm doing push-ups and such it feels weird, and when I ride I tape it more than I need to. I figure that way if something does happen maybe the tape will keep the bones from popping out.

"Put Your Right Foot Out"

At Cheyenne Frontier Days in 2014, Bradley Harter and I were helping Sam Spreadborough with his horse in the chute. She'd been throwing a fit, but had calmed down so we just went to watching the rodeo; I let my guard down for just a minute. In what seemed like a tenth of a second this mare reared up, got her foot outside the chute, and caught me right in the stomach.

The chutes at Cheyenne are pretty high up and she sent me flying off the back of the chutes and down in the dirt where all the guys get ready. I went from standing there behind the chute, to being face first in the dirt. I thought, "What the heck just happened…" Because she'd caught me in the belly I couldn't get my air; I just slowly rocked up on my knees until I got some oxygen in my lungs.

People who were sitting in the first couple of rows had seen the whole thing, and there were a few gasps followed by people inching to the edge of their seats to see if I was alive or not. I'd landed just where the dirt ended and the concrete began.

My hat, sunglasses, and watch were all fine but I didn't feel so fine later that night! How she didn't break any ribs or anything I don't know. My back was really sore though. Sam and Bradley felt terrible; Bradley especially because he's my mentor and has been trying to teach me everything he can. He remembers talking to me about the saddle position and the next second I just wasn't standing there anymore.

I rode the next day and ended up fracturing my foot when I got hung up. The horse ran me along the gate on the way out and things went downhill from there. I can't say my first experience at Cheyenne was the smoothest but it certainly won't be my last!

Clint Craig

Clint Craig is from Nena, Arkansas but makes his home outside Weatherford, Texas.

Clint has been riding bulls since he was 12 years old. Clint's dad rode bulls, which spurred Clint's interest towards bull riding. Bull riding seemed to come naturally to Clint and his family started taking him to junior rodeos.

Clint won several junior titles in Oklahoma, won the Arkansas High School Rodeo Association title his senior year in high school, and won the International Youth Finals Rodeo title that same year.

When Clint graduated from high school he headed towards to professional circuit of the PRCA and the Built Ford Tough Series of the PBR. Clint made the NFR in 2004 and 2007. In 2007 Clint Craig won Cheyenne Frontier Days and the Pendleton Round Up. In 2010 Clint won the National Western in Denver, CO and set the arena record with 93 points.

"The Gambler"

In 2003 I was a fresh-faced 20 year-old, and I was traveling with a guy we'll call Josh O. He was 36 at the time and showing me the ropes out on the road. He was my role model and really helped me learn a lot. In June of that year we were at the Reno, Nevada rodeo. We rode at the rodeo on a Tuesday night, and I had the bull K-78 Unforgiven and Josh had a bull called Major League. Major League and Unforgiven whipped us both out!

Major League got Josh down in the arena dirt and worked him over really well, and Unforgiven threw me off and stepped squarely on my back. You know when you slip on the bathroom rug and your foot just shoots out and slides across the floor with it? Well I was basically the bathroom rug for Unforgiven. When he stepped on my back it whacked my face against the ground so hard that it broke my nose. But then to add injury to insult, he slid with my face against the ground. The road rash I had on my face was unreal, two black eyes, a broke nose, my lips were pretty much just peeled off. That was a horrible night for Josh and I.

So the next morning I wake up and Josh is telling me, "Clint, we gotta go to Vegas!" I was like, "Uh Josh, Vegas really isn't on the way to Greeley from Reno." We were supposed to hang out in Reno one more day and then head north to Greeley, Colorado for a rodeo there.

"We just got to go, man!" I did not want to go to Vegas and told him so. He told me to just come to his hotel room and he'd tell me what was up and why we had to go to Vegas. I slowly got ready, really slowly actually, and ambled over to his hotel room.

As soon as I got into his room I could tell he was in a bit of a panic. He was flying around the room throwing his things together, "Look man, you know how I like to gamble and I gamble too much. Well I've spent all my money gambling and my wife has cut me off from our bank accounts and credit cards. I have $1,000 in a safe at the Gold Coast Casino and that's it. We've got to go to Vegas, get my money, and let me try and double it."

I thought it was completely ridiculous and quickly started trying to talk him down from the idea. "Look man, we really don't need to go down there. I don't want to go down there." He looked at me and said, "Fine, then you can pay all my fees for the 4th of July run."

And just like that we were headed to Vegas.

It's a good eight-hour drive from Reno to Vegas, so we threw our stuff in the truck and took off. We had to be back in Greeley, CO by Friday so we had to hustle. We drove all day, and freaking got pulled over on the way down there. This cop comes sauntering up to the truck, now mind you Josh and I both have black eyes and my face is all torn up. We rolled down the window and his face was that of pure shock, "What happened to you boys?" I just looked at him with a straight face and said, "Well he was running his mouth so we just got out of the truck and beat the shit out of each other." Although the cop thought that was pretty funny, he quickly realized we'd been at the Reno Rodeo. He took pity on us and sent us on our way without a ticket.

Finally we arrived at the Gold Coast in Vegas at about 10pm.

We got to the room, Josh throws his bags on the bed, and just goes "I'll be back later." I felt like hell so I just went to sleep. Woke up the next morning around 8 and realized Josh's bags were exactly where he'd left them; he hadn't been to bed or back to the room yet. I knew this was not a good sign so I jumped up, threw my clothes on, and headed downstairs.

I got down into the casino and started searching for Josh. It didn't take long to spot him at a table across the room and from a distance he looked like he was pitching an absolute fit; he's throwing his arms in the air, pointing, going nuts, and being overly animated. I just shook my head. I figured that I would find him in that kind of shape. I ambled my way over to the table and as soon as I got there he moved to another table. The dealer at the table he was leaving was crying. Poor girl has tears coming down her face.

"Josh, man, what the hell is going on? What just happened?"

He whipped his head around and fired, "That bitch right there just took over a $100,000 from me! I had $100,000 on that table and she took every last penny from me! I've got a house payment to make, things to pay for, and she took all my damn money!"

I was thinking, "Well dude, you gave it to her..." In my mind he'd had the power to leave the table at any time; in his mind it was all her fault. There was no rationalizing with Josh when he was gambling. Josh was dead broke, not a penny to his name. The Gold Coast gave him a $2500 marker and he started back gambling.

At this point I am freaked out, I'm 20 years old and I've never seen anything like this before. I'd heard about it, seen it in movies, but never experienced it in real life. I take off away from the tables and called our friend Myron, who was actually one of Josh's best friends. He was really calm and told me, "Clint, he's going to start winning again. When he starts winning again just reach up on the table and start taking chips from him. Make sure he has enough to gamble with, but he's going to make a comeback eventually. Just keep sticking chips in your pocket and don't let him know you have them."

With those instructions I headed back over to the table and it wasn't long before he started winning again. He was playing two and three hands at a time, and went from $2500 in the hole to now he's gambling $500 chips. I'd never even seen $500 chips! I'm just slowly sliding my hand up on the table and taking these $500 chips. My pocket starts getting really full so I take them out to see how many I've got. You know the "Cowabunga, dude!" sign? Where you extend your pinky and thumb? Between my thumb and my pinky was as full as it could get with $500 chips, $12,500 to be exact."

I didn't have any place else to stuff more chips so I shoved them back in my pockets, my pockets looked like a chipmunk's cheeks. I took off up to the room as fast as I could. I shoved the chips in a sock, hid the sock in the bottom of my bag, and rushed back downstairs. On the way back to the tables I'd called Myron and told him what was going on and how much I'd snuck away already.

"Does he know you have that $12,500?"

"No sir, it's in a sock in my bag."

"Good. DO NOT let him know you have it."

At that point it's about 10:30am and I look over and see Dan Mortenson and I think it was Glen O'Neil standing by the bar. I went over and was like, "Dan, do you see what's going on?" He'd told me he'd watched the initial demise around 5am. Apparently Josh had been up $120,000 at one point and lost it all. I was freaking speechless…$120,000! I couldn't believe what I was hearing or witnessing.

I decided I'd better head back over to the table and start sneaking chips from Josh again. It wasn't long before I had another $12,500 jammed between my pinky and thumb. I took that back up the room, put it in a different sock, and hid it in my bag. I knew we had $25,000 at least, but to be honest, I was starting to get swept up in the craziness. At one point, counting what I'd hidden in the room and what was on the table, we were up to about $50,000.

At one point Josh started getting super belligerent. I kept pestering him that we needed to go, he'd had enough, and he was just becoming a bigger asshole by the moment. We finally ended up standing face to face and I pointed at the pit boss, "Can you kick his ass out of here?" The pit boss informed me that Josh wasn't actually doing anything wrong, "Well what if I punched him? Will you kick him out then?" I knew I needed to get Josh out of there as fast as I could. They threatened to throw me out so I shut up pretty fast.

Well I'm an idiot and I'm getting into this. We ended losing $25,000 but I knew we had $25,000 back in the room. But at 20 years old it was almost too much for me to handle and I'm partially to blame in egging Josh on a bit towards the end. We wound up getting so drunk and tired that Josh finally decided to call it quits.

"Clint, how much money do we have?"

"I'm not telling you!"

We went and ate, and then went up to the room. At this point it's getting on into the afternoon and I know we have to ride in Greeley, Colorado the following afternoon. That was about 16 hours away. Josh is hammered, doesn't even take a shower, and he won't stop hassling me about how much money we have. Finally I broke and told him that we had $25,000. He starts laughing and smiling, "Oh man, what a great day! Yeah buddy!"

At that time you could cash out $9,999 without being taxed so we went downstairs, cashed out that much, put the rest back in the safe at the Gold Coast, hopped in my truck, and took off for Greeley.

I needed to get my oil changed, so we stopped at this place almost right next to the Gold Coast. I was stone cold sober and ready to roll but, Josh's adrenaline high starting to wear off and a drunken stupor is starting to set in. He's drunk, scraggly, smells like alcohol and cigarettes, and is slouched over in this chair next to this poor lady. He passed out and starting snorting inches from her face.

I'll never forget this lady looking at him, looking away, trying to move away form him, looking back at him....finally she just got up and moved across the room. She was so disgusted and I couldn't stop laughing. They finished up with my truck, I basically dragged Josh into the passenger seat, and off we went to Greeley. Josh paid for the oil change, all our fuel, and my entry fees in Greeley "for my troubles".

That was definitely an experience I'll never forget, especially being 20 years old and seeing that kind of cash. I've never seen anything like that before and I know I most likely won't ever witness something like that again.

"Taking A Ride On The Carousel"

About February of 2006 I was traveling with my buddy Logan. We were supposed to fly out at like 9:30 on a Saturday morning to go to Florida and ride in an Extreme Bull Riding event. Late on Friday night I got a call from the airlines that our flight had been cancelled, and they'd rescheduled us for a flight that departed Saturday night at 10pm. There has been an infamous Texas ice storm and the airport had all but shut down.

That was unacceptable; the bull riding was going to be over by the time we got there! We had to be there by at least 6pm to even have a chance of making the event on time.

I called Logan, filled him in on what was going on, and promised I'd find a way. I start calling airlines, looking online, and every flight is grounded. Nothing is flying out, and if it is it's not headed anywhere near Florida. I decided that the next morning we'd go to the Dallas/Fort Worth Airport and try to get on something going standby to Florida. We just had to take the risk.

We drove to DFW the next morning in the ice storm. The roads were so slick, I remember us sliding sideways across an overpass right near downtown. We finally made it to the airport and everything is shut down, zero flights going anywhere. What do you do when you're stuck in an airport with no hope of leaving anytime soon? You head to the bar.

It's about 10am and we just start drinking. We met an older couple who introduced us to the Irish Car Bomb. The couple was drinking them like they were nothing. The man insisted on buying us one of them and one turned into quite a few. You know how that goes.... we were having one hell of a time in the airport.

Finally we ended up getting on the 10pm flight the airline had originally rebooked for us. Logan and I were solidly drunk off Irish Car Bombs, so we slept the whole way to Orlando. We woke up when we landed and despite our bar adventures, felt pretty good. We shuffled off the plane and headed towards the baggage claim. As soon as we arrived in the baggage claim area I started getting a little restless. There were multiple baggage claim carousels just going round and round.

"Hey! Hey, Logan! Just do what I do, okay?"

With that I sat down Indian style on the baggage claim with Logan right behind me. I just decided, "Screw it, we're going in the back." Logan and I just ducked our heads down and go breezing through the baggage claim flaps and back into the baggage area. It was like being in the Land of Oz, we were back there where no one else got to go, no one else had ever seen!

We're just going along, there are bags everywhere, knowing full well we are not supposed to be back there. There's a group of guys standing in a circle, one guy conducting a meeting, and they're standing about a foot away from the carousel. I mean I could have reached out and grabbed this guy's leg and he was clueless that we were there. We're just going by and as soon as we get dead even with them I yelled, "Hey! Y'all get back to work!" You would have thought I started firing a gun off, those guys jumped six feet in the air and started screaming.

"Hey! You're not supposed to be back here!"

"Well...we are!"

They're not doing anything but screaming at us and Logan and

I are in hysterics. We think this is the greatest idea we've ever had. As we came back through the flaps to come out, it was like we were being birthed into the world, the look on peoples' faces when two cowboys came through the baggage claim flaps was priceless.

Logan and I just stood up like nothing was going on, completely expressionless, stepped off the baggage claim, and starting walking over to our baggage claim. (We'd realized this wasn't even our baggage claim carousel.)

People were laughing and gawking at us as we sauntered away. After a couple minutes of standing at our baggage claim, I realize there are security guards and police officers strategically placing themselves around us; one was over in the corner, two were eerily close behind us. All of a sudden they just converged on us like a pack of wolves.

The no-nonsense woman storms up to me and goes, "Gentleman, can we see your IDs?" We just tried to play it cool, "Um, is there a problem here ma'am?" She barked back, "Didn't you boys just ride the baggage carousel around, through the back and such?" Logan is snickering and I can feel a smirk coming across my face, "Well yes ma'ma, we did do that."

Turns out that's considered a breach of national security, something which didn't seem to dawn on me until the lady was in my face and I was surrounded by security guards. Since 9/11 though I guess it should've crossed my mind but I blame the Irish Car Bombs.

At that moment I suddenly sobered up and got really scared. A breach of national security? I knew that more than likely we were in big trouble. We'd just been goofing off, having some fun, and the consequences hadn't even entered my mind. Here we were just having some fun and now I was certain we were about to go to jail.

They take us back to a little room and start questioning us. They're calling the FBI and I'm simultaneously calling my lawyer. I told him what we'd done and he assured me not to worry about it. He wasn't surprised by my actions, "You didn't do anything wrong. Just be a gentleman, answer their questions, and they should let you go. If they don't, call me back and we'll get it taken care of."

Logan and I just continued with our usual "Yes ma'am" and "Yes sir", that's one time I was grateful I'd be raised with manners. After we answered airport security's questions, they put us on the phone with the FBI.

The brisk man on the other end of the line was far from happy with what we'd done. We went back through the story; I'd admitted what we'd done, apologized, and he was questioning about my record.

"Why do you have so many speeding tickets?"

"Well sir, I tend to drive too fast. I'm always in a hurry. I'm really sorry."

Aside from my speeding tickets my rap sheet is clean, Logan on the other hand, has a few drunk and disorderly charges from his young rodeo career.

"Son, can you tell me about your record?

Logan rattled off his charges and there was a pause on the other end of the line.

"Son, are you sure that's all?"

"Um yes sir, that's pretty much all I can think of." Logan was starting to look worried.

"Well what about this charge here?" and the FBI agent spouted off some charge that Logan has forgotten about. Logan admitted he forgot about it and the FBI man started accusing him of lying to him and hiding things from him. This went back and forth for about three different charges Logan forgot about.

"Son, have you noticed a common denominator in all these things? All these problems you've had? All the run-ins with the law?"

Logan just bluntly answered, "Yes sir, I was drunk when all these things happened."

"Son, maybe you ought to think about not drinking!"

Logan said he'd take it into consideration from now on and they let us go. Our buddies came and picked us up from the airport, we missed the bull riding, rode at the rodeo the next day, and for the life of me I can't remember what happened the next day at the rodeo.

"Hit Baby"

It was October of 2008, we were pregnancy checking cows and vaccinating them; just the standard fall check-up stuff. I grew up on a ranch, my dad runs right at 500 head of momma cows and my grandfather runs about 120 head.

I'd worked thousands of cattle in the corral in my lifetime; it might even be more than thousands. There's an alleyway leading up to the chutes, it's about 10 foot wide and funnels down into a chute. I was sorting the cows out one at a time and herding them down into the chute.

My grandfather runs ranker cows. They're bred with some attitude, big horns, and they're smart. They're not bad, they're snorty and you just have to be on your toes around them. This cow, she had flat horns about a foot long on each side, turned back on me as I was driving her up the ally. I just stepped to her, hollered at her, and waited for her to move back. I'd known this cow forever; she wasn't especially a sour one. She still wasn't moving so I hit her on the nose with the sorting paddle, and apparently that was enough to make her a different cow.

She came towards me and I just made a round around her and jumped up on the fence. When I jumped up on the fence I was just going to spring up and over the fence. Well when my foot hit the fence, she hit my foot and both my legs shoot between the bars of the corral. I was stuck and she just hooked the shit out my lower body for a few seconds to prove her point.

I felt this pain the first hit she took, but after that my adrenaline kicked in a bit. Guys were hollering at her and finally she goes and leaves me alone. I pulled myself up enough to see that she'd shredded both my pants legs; they were just ripped to pieces. I went ahead and finished climbing over the fence and hopped down landing on my feet.

I knew from riding bulls for so long when I'm hurt and when I'm not. It happens enough you can usually tell what you can walk off versus what needs medical attention. As soon as I landed I knew something was wrong. I called some guys over to me and tried to figure out what was wrong. About 10 inches above my knee, up near where my groin muscle is, in between my hamstring and my groin, is a hole that looked like a 270 exit wound.

As soon as I was standing the blood started pouring out of my leg and running down what was left of my pants. It was coming out like a steady stream of water, like if you turned a water bottle on its side and just let the water flow out. It's just pouring out. I put my hand over it and went to limping. Our vet, Randy Burgess, was standing there and I went, "Randy, I'm hurt. I think we need to go to the hospital....now."

Randy asked me to let him see so I moved my hand over just enough so that he could see; "Yep, let's go, right now." Another guy was helping us, his name was Brandon, and he wanted a look at it too. He'd seen his fair share of wounds, he was a hog hunter and people get hooked a lot. I really pulled my pants to the side this time and took my hand completely off, "Holy shit! We have to go NOW. Let's go! Hurry!"

I was limping to the truck, just as calm as could be, with Brandon and Randy on either side of me. My grandfather was about 77 or 78 at that time. He'd had a lot of surgeries and is probably the toughest human being I know. He motioned for us to all stop, "Now Clint, now everyone, let's just calm down! Let's go up to the house and get you some crackers and water." I'm bleeding like I have a gunshot wound and he wanted me to go up to the house for crackers and water. It was all I could do not to mouth off, "What are we going to do? Make a paste?" I bit my tongue though.

I calmly just went, "No, I think I'm going to go to the hospital on this one." I got over to the truck, reached up to grab the door, and the door was locked. Up to that point I was feeling fine, I don't know if it was the disappointment of me being unable to sit down or the blood pouring all over the place, but I went white as a sheet and almost passed out. I had to mentally check myself, got my breath going, and Randy unlocked the truck so I could climb in.

Once I was in the truck I tied a piggin string around my leg and tied it off as tight as I could. I grabbed some gauze which was fortunately in the truck, and shoved it up in the hole as far as I could. I knew the dangers of having your femoral artery severed; I knew you could bleed to death. What I didn't know is whether it was cut or not; the blood was just pouring out of my leg instead of squirting so I took that as a good sign.

So we hauled ass to the hospital. I called them when we were en route so they were waiting on me when I got there. Because I'd been gored by this nasty ol' cow horn, they wanted to put me under and go in my leg and really clean it out for bacteria before closing the hole up. They put me to sleep and did the surgery in about 45 minutes.

Turns out the hole was three inches deep, it went in between my groin and hamstring muscle, and had missed my femoral artery by half an inch. They stitched the hole shut and left a tube in it so it could drain. I spent three days in the hospital on IV antibiotics and getting blood transfusions. I lost 2 units of blood total, which is about a quarter of your body's total blood content. A unit is about a pint and you're supposed to have 8-10 units of blood in your body; do the math. If I hadn't gone to the hospital I would have most likely slowly bled to death.

To this day, if I don't drink enough water or if I sit down for a really long time and then go to stand up, that spot feels like there's bugs in there. I guess it's scar tissue and nerve damage, but it feels incredibly weird. It feels like it's walking and I'm not.

When I was in the hospital they finished preg checking and such and ending up cutting that cow's horns. Brandon brought me about a 3 1/2" piece of her horn to the hospital. I still have those horns in my house.

Turns out the crackers and water wouldn't have done much good, much to my grandfather's dismay.

"Trespassers"

June 2010, the weekend of Union, Oregon, Sisters, Oregon, and Livermore, California, Artie Myer and I were traveling together. We flew in and met up with a couple guys so we could all travel together. We went to Union, went to Sisters, and drove all night from Sisters to the afternoon performance in Livermore the next day.

After Livermore, Artie, Wes, and Garrett went one way and they other guys split and went another direction. My group was going up to Don Kish's place to pick out some heifers to buy. That night we drove the five-hour drive from Livermore, CA to Red Bluff, CA.

I'd been at the ranch once before so I thought I knew the lay of the land and such. Don's place was really nice. When we got there we just pulled up by the bull pens and I called Don up. He told me to go ahead and take the guys to the bunkhouse; he wasn't sure if anyone else would be in there but we should just go in and make ourselves at home. He assured me he'd be out in the morning and we'd start looking at cows.

Like I said, I'd been there before so when he offered up directions to the bunkhouse I turned him down. I thought I knew where it was and we'd be fine. We drove across the canal back to where I thought the bunkhouse was.

So we walk up and into the bunkhouse, we walked up on the screened-in back porch, through the back door, through a sort of washroom, and into the kitchen. Through the kitchen I could see a man and a woman sitting on the couch. Kish had told he didn't know who would be there and to just make ourselves at home; so that's what I was doing.

I walked into the kitchen, "Hey! Hello! We're here!" About that time this blue heeler comes streaking in to the kitchen and starts nipping at me. I jumped up on the kitchen counter and was hugging my legs to my chest and this little shit is still trying to come after me.

This guy walks into the kitchen, never calling the dog off, flips on the lights, and goes, "Hey guys, how's it going? Don't worry about that dog, he won't get you!" With that the dog sat and continued to watch me with a look that assured me my feet better stay out of range of his teeth. The man continued, "What are you boys doing?"

I'd never seen this guy before in my life. I figured he was a ranch hand or something, so I just tried to strike up a conversation and be mannerly to him. After we exchanged a few pleasantries we explained that Don had told us just to come on in and make ourselves at home.

"Yeah, y'all looking for the Kish ranch?"

"Uh yes sir, are we in the wrong place?"

"Yes sir, you boys are in the wrong house. The Kish ranch is just across the canal over there."

I quickly realized I'd made a mistake in thinking I knew where we were supposed to go, "Oh man, I'm so sorry!" I was just trying to explain and falling all over myself for intruding.

The man slowly raised a finger and said, "Hold on there boys, I want to show you something." He goes back into the living room and I can see him from where I'm still sitting on the counter. The rest of the guys and I are exchanging some uneasy glances of embarrassment and a growing feeling of discomfort.

I saw this guy reach down and pick up an SKS rifle from beside the couch. I wasn't scared at this point; I thought he was just going to explain that around there people have guns in the house, so we needed to be more careful in the future. Well, I watch this guy amble towards me. He got about five feet away from me, chambered a bullet, and pointed this rifle right at my head.

"The first thing you can do is get the hell off my counter. The second thing you boys can do is get the hell out of my house."

With that I felt the blood drain from my face.

Artie went to take off running because he thought this guy was going to shoot us all. The man swung the rifle towards Artie, "Hold it right there! You boys are going to walk out of here really nice and real slow, you understand me?"

Wes, being the cool character that he is, started laughing and shrugged his shoulders, "You serious, dude?"

The man moved the gun from Artie to Wes, "Yeah I'm serious, get the hell out of here right now." At this point I decided to crawl down off the counter and start making my way towards the back door. Things had just gotten really real; it was like a bad dream. I knew he'd chambered a bullet and I was just feet away from the gun. I was the first one in the house and was on my way to being the last one out, as they other guys had slowly exited.

I looked over my shoulder on my way out the door, and this SKS rifle was a foot from my back. I'd shot a SKS before and all I could think about was how sharp those bullets were and how much it was going to hurt when he shot me in the back. My whole back was just tense; I kept bracing for the impact the whole way out of the house.

We all finally made it out on the porch and were heading towards the van and this guy is still "escorting" us off his property. We'd all been drinking beers, we weren't drunk, but we'd been drinking beers. He must have picked up on it because he said, "Hey, you boys have anymore of those beers?"

Thinking this was a twisted peace offering, considering he still had a rifle pointed at me, I chimed up, "Yeah! We have a whole cooler full! You can have my beer, man!" I was just breathing a sigh of relief because I thought the joke was up and this was going to be okay.

Without seemingly moving his lips this guy goes, "I don't want your fucking beer, y'all get the hell off my place." In that moment the blood drained from my face for the second time. We all quickly hustled off the porch, out into the yard, and backed our way to the van. The second we got in the van we locked the doors and it was straight up a scene from "Dukes of Hazzard", spinning gravel and hauling ass. We were all terrified.

We're driving back towards the bull pens and see the real bunkhouse. We pulled up there and started cracking doors and peeking through windows to make sure it was empty. We went through every room making sure there wasn't anyone we were going to surprise and have shoot us.

We shuffled back out to the driveway and we all have the adrenaline shakes. We literally drop in the gravel and we're trying to slow our heart rates down. I'm just shaking like a leaf. I occasionally smoke cigarettes from time to time so I break out a cigarette; took me a minute to get it lit because my hand was shaking so badly. Artie, who never smoked a cigarette, went, "Clint, let me have one of them cigarettes!" In hindsight, I'm not sure Artie didn't pee himself a little bit throughout the ordeal.

I wound up having really bad dreams that night, couldn't ever seem to fall asleep and when I did it was just terrible nightmares, almost like night terrors. The next morning Kish told us he was surprised that guy hadn't shot and killed us; apparently he was certified clinically crazy and had quite the trigger happy finger. He couldn't believe we'd made it out of there alive, and to be honest I can't believe we did either.

Luke Butterfield

Luke is a 6x Canadian National Finals qualifier in saddle bronc and was the 2012 Canadian National Finals Saddle Bronc Champion.

Luke turned pro in 2005 when he was 20 years old.

When Luke isn't traveling he's helping work cattle on his family's ranch in Ponoka, Alberta. He hopes to make the Wrangler National Finals Rodeo in 2015.

"Textbook Perfect"

In July 2011, I was up at the Calgary Stampede. Being from Canada, the Stampede is a huge deal. I know it's important to other cowboys too, but being Canadian makes it all the more special to me.

I'd made it to the short go on Sunday, directly out of my pool vying for the wild card spot. With that one wild card spot you have a chance at $100,000 in one ride.

I couldn't believe I made it; the realization was almost beyond me. It was kind of like, "Holy cow, this is happening."

Going into that day I just relaxed, or tried to. I just went about my day like I would any other day. All four of us, Bradley Harter, Jesse Wright, Chad Ferley, and myself headed to the stage to draw our horses. Chad had won a world title already. Bradley and Jesse had been to the NFR I don't know how many times.

Not only was I trying to ride for $100,000, but I was also riding against three of the best saddle bronc riders in the world. Somehow that didn't mess with my head like many would've expected. My mental state was just on point. I wish I could be in that mental state all the time.

I drew first and drew a horse that I didn't know too well. I knew he'd won the world already, so that was a confidence booster. To me, at the time, it didn't really complicate my draw. The rest of the guys drew their horses and then we hustled back to the chutes where the horses were already waiting.

It all happened so fast, I didn't even get a chance to watch the other guys' outs. I was last to ride. I remember I was getting ready and I heard them announce Chad Ferley's score of 92 points; it actually might have been higher than that.

I remember getting on and it was just like another ride. Adjusting everything so I felt ready, trying not to think what all was at stake within this 8 second period. I was definitely nervous, but no more than I'd experienced anywhere else.

Just the feeling though, the feeling that I was riding for $100,000, the Calgary sun beating down on the area, and an unknown horse beneath me; it's hard to put that into words. I was squatting down in the chute and Dustin Flundra was helping me get set. He leaned down and said, "Take him, get it right, this is for $100,000." In that moment things really sunk it. It was just a mental check of what all was at stake.

We rolled the horse, I just wanted to go out there and get it done before I started overthinking things.

That was probably one of the best bronc rides I've ever made. It felt amazing; I wish it could feel like that every time. I heard the buzzer and got off and this massive smile broke out across my face. Beating a guy who was 92 seemed impossible, but as soon as my boots hit the dirt I had a feeling that it might happen.

I ended up scoring 90, winning second, and just missing out on the $100,000. I wasn't one bit disappointed at all though; it was one of the greatest experiences of my rodeo career so far.

I don't know how to describe the feeling of that ride though; it just felt textbook perfect. I'm really hard on myself, I'm a perfectionist when it comes to bucking horses. It just worked that day. Everything worked perfect that day, between making the draw and the textbook ride, so 2nd place didn't feel too bad.

Most guys would say there was a small part of them that was upset but I wasn't; I was so happy with what had happened. Even just being there on the final Sunday and having the opportunity. Not many cowboys get that opportunity and I had not only been given it, but had made the most of it. Chad just deserved to win that day. Maybe if my horse had been just a little stronger it would've changed things, but things played out exactly how they were supposed to.

That feeling though, of a bronc ride so smooth and perfect; that's something that doesn't happen often. Only one other ride has ever clicked like that. It was also 90 points, but unfortunately only for a $1500 payout.

I won something like $37,000 at Calgary that year, which was the biggest check I've ever won at a rodeo. That one ride was like $25,000, which was the best 8-second workday I'd ever had!

That feeling I had though, from knowing I'd made the $100,000 round to what felt like a flawless ride, to everything wrapping up, it was just great. My mom and dad were there and lots of people from around Alberta, so that made it even sweeter. That was really the first major rodeo they ever saw me at. That was before the Canadian National Finals.

I always remember watching that final Sunday on TV growing up; they televise the final Sunday every year. I always dreamed of being in that showdown round for the $100,000. Just to have that actually happen, and have my parents there, I'd dreamed about that day for a long time. To be fortunate enough to have that opportunity, that was awesome. I'll never forget that.

Hannah Montey

Hannah Montey has been raising and training horses since 2002.

She graduated from Colorado State University with a degree in Sociology.

Hannah has been rodeoing professionally since 2005, as well as breeding and training horses. Some of her favorite rodeos are the Greeley Stampede, Rooftop Rodeo in Estes Park, the National Western Stock Show in Denver, and Cheyenne Frontier Days. Hannah has a fine collection of Quarter Horses and Thoroughbred crosses to train and run in both barrel futurities and professional rodeos.

"There is no substitute or secondary feeling quite like the blood-rush of a competition run under the arena lights and amidst the rodeo atmosphere. The hard work we all put into this sport is paid off in every victory lap we earn. Its a must feel personally kind of thing to truly appreciate the addiction."

"One Run"

Growing up in the area around Denver, there are four rodeos we have religiously gone to; Estes Park, Greeley, Denver (National Western), and Cheyenne. My family doesn't rodeo, I don't come from a rodeo family. I wasn't brought up in it, nothing was given to me, and I had to learn a lot on my own. It's always been a personal passion.

My parents always had horses for fun but I was enamored with them. I was the little kid at the rodeos with her face plastered up against the fence watching the girls warm up their barrel horses. I was just hooked from a very young age and knew that rodeo and horses were going to be part of my life.

My most memorable moment competing, the game changer if you will, was at the National Western Stock Show in Denver in 2008. I had a good mare that I'd been running. This was the third or fourth time I'd entered, and I felt confident about things. My mare had been working great, and I didn't see any reason to take a risk and not run my good horse. I've run her for 10 years now, we just have a connection and I've always stuck with that.

Long story short, Round 1 comes along and this mare ran well, but she wasn't fast enough. There was no way I was going to be in the money if she continued to run like that. My whole family was there and it was just incredibly disappointing. That night at dinner my sister asked me if I was going to win it or just be content making good runs without being in the money.

I sat and thought about it a little bit; I had a five-year-old mare with me too. Agonys Chick Delight, or Ginger, was well bred and a horse you couldn't take your eyes off. She hadn't competed much, maybe had made 10 runs to date. She was extremely athletic and I knew she'd mature into an incredible barrel horse. Our family motto has always been "Go big or go home" so I figured I might as well see how the young mare did against some of the best in the event.

So Round 2 comes along and this little mare goes out and runs the 4th fastest time of the round, we were just short of making the short round. My first run had been good, just too slow to get me back in the short. In the barrel world tenths of a seconds matter more than anyone realizes. This little mare who barely had 10 runs on her ran the same pattern four-tenths of a second faster than my best horse.

It was just an amazing experience to be able to be part of the victory lap at the end of the go round. It's such a solid feeling of accomplishment to be able to step off that little mare and go, "THAT'S why we do this! This right here!" A lot of young horses take a considerable amount of time to get their confidence, but this little mare had run like she'd been doing it for years.

That experience was so rewarding for me, especially when it comes to training barrel horses. There are a lot of good jackpot barrel horses that won't win a dime in rodeo; it's a totally different game. It takes a very specific, very special kind of horse to go out and run well at rodeos; it's a whole different set of circumstances. For a young horse to come out and run like she did, with the music and the lights, I was bursting with pride.

It's funny; five girls in my round had been to the NFR before. I was mentally telling myself that if this young mare just made a solid run that would be fantastic. But to be able to out run some of those girls, get my $100 gift certificate, take a victory lap, it was all just a great experience. Later, I parked up next to the arena rail and signed some autographs and let kids take pictures, and again this mare handled it like a champ.

I hope that helped motivate kids, especially the ones who haven't had rodeo experience or don't have a rodeo background. I don't think rodeo is a dying sport, if anything I think it's a growing sport. You just have to enlighten people and help teach the next generation about connecting with a horse and the great benefits that come from that.

I felt like things had really clicked with that mare that day, between the run and interacting with fans and kids afterwards. That whole experience was just a great reminder of why I do what I do, why I love running barrels, and why I love the sport of rodeo just as much as I did when I was little.

Ned Pepper Stewart

Ned grew up in Central Texas on his family's farm, which dates back to the 1800s. Ned began fighting and riding bulls when he was 12 in a makeshift pen his family built for him.

In 2001 Ned left the professional rodeo lifestyle and settled down with his family in North Texas where he has a small cattle operation.

Ned occasionally competes in working ranch horse competitions and judges a few bullfighting competitions. During his downtime Ned enjoys team penning and ranch sorting events. He also the host of "Texas Ranch N Rodeo Weekly", a weekly internet talk show featuring cowboys, ranchers, and people involved in the sport of rodeo.

"Dealer's Choice"

I was working as a bullfighter at an event in the northern part of Texas. It was probably sometime in the 90's, though I can't exactly recall when.

As a way to entertain the crowd we set up a game of bull poker in the middle of the arena. Basically, you set up a game of poker, table and all, and then turn a bull out simultaneously. So we got the table set up, all the players were seated around the table, and they turned this bull out. It was my job to get the bull's attention and direct him towards the table and other bullfighters.

This bull wasn't really a fighting bull, he was a broad bucking bull; he'd hook you a little bit, but generally needed some persuasion to be more aggressive. He wasn't too interested initially so I ran over and jumped up on the table to try and catch his attention and draw him towards the game.

As soon as I jumped up on the table I realized that it wasn't the sturdiest thing in the world; it's wobbling all around and sinking into the sand as I move around on it. The middle keeps sinking where I'm standing and I realize it's probably going to break into 20 pieces at any given moment.

Unfortunately for me, my jumping up on the table had indeed drawn the bull's attention to the players and myself. The first pass he made the bull clipped a guy on the edge and jostled the table a bit more. It was still wobbling back and forth with me on top on it.

At that point I realized there was no way I could jump off this table that was swaying and buckling and run interference for the other guys, I'd most likely hurt myself just trying to get off the table. As soon as I came to the realization that I was basically stuck on top of this table, the bull turned to me, stared me down for a minute, and then came straight for me.

I quickly realized I needed an exit strategy and fast. My options were extremely limited, so being a bullfighter, I decided to take a risk. As the bull charged toward me, lowering his head for impact, I just stepped up on the back of his neck, walked (halfway ran) down his back and jumped onto the ground. It's a move that many bullfighters try to make but they usually end up getting hurt. In the briefest moment, I had accomplished this move and somehow gotten myself out of harm's way. The crowd loved it, they went wild, whooping and hollering for me! I think they thought it was my plan the whole time, which certainly hadn't been the case.

Afterwards, once the bull had been returned to his pen and the rodeo had come to an end, we were signing autographs and taking pictures with fans. A little kid ran up to me with a massive grin on his dirt-smudged face. He said that watching me walk down that bull's back was the coolest thing he'd ever seen. Just seeing how much he'd enjoyed it and how fired up he was about bullfighting, that was extremely gratifying to me.

That's what it's all about, keeping the contestants safe and entertaining the crowd. We'd given them what they'd wanted to see and all the bull riders were safe.

Kelly Barrett

Kelly Barrett is originally from Cannon Falls, Minnesota but makes his home in Arizona.

Kelly competed in high school rodeo, but decided not to turn pro when he turned 18. Kelly makes his living as a farrier. In his spare time he likes to rope competitively and train horses.

"My first word was horse, is that weird? That's weird. It should be mom or dad or something, but for me it was horse."

"Welcome To The Business"

When I was a kid it was my job to hold the horses for the farrier. I was cool with that, it gave me someone to talk to and they put up with me.

As soon as I turned 19 I moved to Arizona and I thought I was going to be a horse trainer. I was convinced that was how I was going to make a living. That was fine for a while but one day the farrier showed up and he blew my mind. The shoes were grinded, the hoof was all clean and smooth, and everything was just unbelievable.

"Holy crap, I need to do this!" I thought.

I never knew that it could be such an art really. In Minnesota we were always the last stop of the day and our farrier never seemed to put much effort into things. He got the job done, but after being under 30 horses a day he would hobble around our place and he wasn't especially chatty. When I saw a real farrier work and saw the possibilities in it, I started investigating.

First, I saw the bill the guy left which pretty much blew my mind. He was done by noon, didn't have to come back for six weeks, and he'd just made bank. I started asking him about his prices and realized he'd given me a smoking deal all things considered. Secondly, my neighbor is also a farrier so I tried to borrow his tools and teach myself which was an epic failure.

Finally, I looked up a horseshoeing school back in Minnesota. It was near my mom's work, my dad was willing to help me pay for it so long as I shod his horses for free, so off I went. Initially I was just planning on learning the trade to save myself some money by taking care of my own horses without crippling them. I never expected it to turn into the business that it has.

After I got out of school I apprenticed under a farrier back in Minnesota for the summer. I didn't get paid back then but I sure learned a lot. It was a good way to practice under a watchful eye. I moved to Arizona and started trying to build a client base, slowly and steadily. Performance horses are great horses and it provides me with steady business.

However, it didn't start out so smoothly, which leads me to the story of my first paying customer.

I was still back in Minnesota, working as an apprentice and shoeing my dad's horses. The guy I was working under promised to get me some clients and two months into things I still had never been paid a dime by anyone all summer long. I was getting super frustrated, not to mention super broke.

One day, out of the blue, this lady calls me. She's a first time horse owner and had just bought this horse from a ranch in Montana. She wanted shoes put on him and I was like, "Yeah, no problem, I'm your huckleberry." It was early in the week so we set things up for that Saturday afternoon. I was so excited all week, just hustling towards the weekend and my first paying client.

Saturday comes and I'm so ready for this. I get up early, which is not my favorite thing to do, make sure everything is packed and perfect. I even had clean and ironed clothes on, and I got to this barn like an hour early. I set up my stuff and I think I am just super professional. I had like this plastic toolbox of tools, but I made that thing look like it was the most professional set-up there ever was.

I sat there and waited for this lady to show up…and waited…and waited. It felt like forever but in reality she was probably only an hour or so late. Finally she pulls in and out jumps four little kids. These kids were little hellions from the second they got out of the car! They're running around like maniacs, playing with a football, and screaming. They instantly dove for my tools and I was all but smacking them away from everything.

She's hollering over these kids that she's going to go catch the horse and she'll be right back. A few minutes later here she comes. I look over and I just go, "Oh shit." She's heading towards me with a 15.2h, 1200lb "ranch horse" who's just breathing fire like a damn dragon. I am searching this horse for any inkling that it's even been ridden, handled, had shoes… anything to give me a peace of mind. I got nothing. This horse is blowing, snorting, and just trembling.

"Shit."

So we get him tied up to the fence, she swore he tied, and this horse is just tense as can be. I slowly ease around him and got him trimmed up. As soon as I get his back foot set up and am going to slip under it, these kids kicked their football and it came straight towards this horse. I quickly got out from under his backend right about the time this horse kicked that ball up into the rafters. He kicked that ball like a damn NFL kicker!

Well, when he kicked he jumped forward and then sucked back; he damn near pulled the walls down. He broke the log railing and took off with the log attached to him. Now he's not only running because of the ball, he's trying to run away from this log that is freaking attached to him.

Finally we got him cornered and caught. I turned to her and was like, "You're going to have to make these kids go play outside or this isn't going to go well." I was trying to be as polite as possible but I was furious; this horse was already jumpy enough and now it was about 10x worse. She hustled the kids outside, where they proceeded to play right outside the barn doors, and we attempted round two.

She quickly decided we didn't need to put shoes on his hind end and man, I sure didn't argue with her. I went to shaping his front shoes. I got the shoe just right, and crossed my fingers. I just kept telling myself that this was my first paying client and I just needed to get the job done.

Finally, I go to get this shoe on his front foot and I have his hoof between my knees and I go to tap this nail in really slowly. He was twitching and dancing around a lot, so in my rookie state I thought, "Oh, well, I'll just give this nail one good whack and hit it out of the park and we'll be done."

As soon as I went to hit the nail, he flinched, I hit the shoe, and this horse came UNCORKED. He jerks his hoof forward and hooks this nail that's halfway in his foot through my chaps, now we're connected. He launches forward, runs this lady over, she lets go, and he takes off with me attached to him.

I'm scrambling trying to rip my chaps, unhook myself, anything I can do. I'm hooked backwards and he's running full steam ahead. He's trying to cow kick the kids in the yard on the way. Halfway down the driveway I finally come loose and land on the side of the driveway; my hammer is still in my hand and I was shaking like a leaf. This horse keeps on running and heads straight down the road.

"Holy shit."

I couldn't even believe what had just happened; I seriously thought I was going to die. I'm just sitting there dumbfounded and here comes this horse back towards the barn. He runs past me, past all the screaming children, and back into the barn. I'm not sure how I stood up or walked back to the barn, my legs were shaking like mad.

I headed back in there, caught him somehow, and just stuck him in the nearest pasture. This lady is sitting in the hallway and her leg and ankle is already swollen and turning black and blue, it was definitely broken. I helped her sort the hellions into the car and packed my stuff up while she called the hospital. I'm sitting there still shaking and she pulls up next to me and rolls down her window.

"How much do I owe you for a trim?"

I just shook her off, "Oh don't worry about it, you're going to have to go pay a hospital bill now." She insisted and to be honest, I could barely think, I just stammered out, "Um, I don't know, like $25? Is that too much?" She writes me a check, thrusts it in my face, and is gone before I know it.

I climb in the cab of my truck and sweat it just pouring off of me. I'm trying to look at this check and my hands are shaking so badly I can't even read the damn thing. Finally, I pull myself together and look at it, all $25 freaking dollars and no tip.

"Welcome to the business, cowboy. You're a farrier now."

I didn't have a scratch on me, which was a miracle, but man, talk about a rough first out. I just hoped that it wasn't always going to be that way and I've kept on with it. Luckily that lady never called me again; can't say I really missed her business.

46635544R00098

Made in the USA
Lexington, KY
10 November 2015